FIVE LECTURES
ON
PSYCHO-ANALYSIS

By SIGMUND FREUD

THE STANDARD EDITION

OF THE COMPLETE PSYCHOLOGICAL WORKS OF

SIGMUND FREUD

24 VOLUMES

Sigmund Freud

FIVE LECTURES
ON
PSYCHO-ANALYSIS

TRANSLATED AND EDITED BY

James Strachey

WITH A BIOGRAPHICAL
INTRODUCTION BY

Peter Gay

W·W·NORTON & COMPANY

New York · London

Library of Congress Cataloging in Publication Data
Freud, Sigmund, 1856–1939
Five lectures on psycho-analysis.
Translation of Über Psychoanalyse.
Bibliography: p.
Includes index.
1. Psychoanalysis—Addresses, essays, lectures.
1. Title. [DNLM: 1. Psychoanalysis. WM460
F889fi]
BF173.F6784   1977   150'.19'52   77-8778

ISBN 0-393-00847-9
ISBN 978-0-393-00847-0

W. W. Norton & Company, Inc. is also the publisher of The Standard Edition
of the Complete Psychological Works of Sigmund Freud.

W. W. Norton & Company, Inc.
500 Fifth Avenue, New York, N.Y. 10110
www.wwnorton.com

W. W. Norton & Company Ltd.
Castle House, 75/76 Wells Street, London W1T 3QT

PRINTED IN THE UNITED STATES OF AMERICA

5 6 7 8 9 0

Contents

SIGMUND FREUD: A BRIEF LIFE
by Peter Gay

It was Freud's fate, as he observed not without pride, to "agitate the sleep of mankind." Half a century after his death, it seems clear that he succeeded far better than he expected, though in ways he would not have appreciated. It is commonplace but true that we all speak Freud now, correctly or not. We casually refer to oedipal conflicts and sibling rivalry, narcissism and Freudian slips. But before we can speak that way with authority, we must read his writings attentively. They repay reading, with dividends.

Sigmund Freud was born on May 6, 1856, in the small Moravian town of Freiberg.[1] His father, Jacob Freud, was an impecunious merchant; his mother, Amalia, was handsome, self-assertive, and young—twenty years her husband's junior and his third wife. Jacob Freud had two sons from his first marriage who were about Amalia Freud's age and lived nearby. One of these half brothers had a son, John, who, though Sigmund Freud's nephew, was older than his uncle.

---

[1] His given names were Sigismund Schlomo, but he never used his middle name and, after experimenting with the shorter form for some time, definitively adopted the first name Sigmund—on occasion relapsing into the original formulation—in the early 1870s, when he was a medical student at the University of Vienna. Freiberg, now in Czechoslovakia, bears the Czech name "Pribor."

Freud's family constellation, then, was intricate enough to puzzle the clever and inquisitive youngster. Inquisitiveness, the natural endowment of children, was particularly marked in him. Life would provide ample opportunity to satisfy it.

In 1860, when Freud was almost four, he moved with his family to Vienna, then a magnet for many immigrants. This was the opening phase of the Hapsburg Empire's liberal era. Jews, only recently freed from onerous taxes and humiliating restrictions on their property rights, professional choices, and religious practices, could realistically harbor hopes for economic advancement, political participation, and a measure of social acceptance. This was the time, Freud recalled, when "every industrious Jewish school boy carried a Cabinet Minister's portfolio in his satchel."[2] The young Freud was encouraged to cultivate high ambitions. As his mother's first-born and a family favorite, he secured, once his family could afford it, a room of his own. He showed marked gifts from his first school days, and in his secondary school, or Gymnasium, he was first in his class year after year.

In 1873, at seventeen, Freud entered the University of Vienna. He had planned to study law, but, driven on by what he called his "greed for knowledge," instead matriculated in the faculty of medicine, intending to embark, not on a conventional career as a physician, but on philosophical-scientific investigations that might solve some of the great riddles that fascinated him. He found his work in physiology and neurology so absorbing that he did not take his degree until 1881.

A brilliant researcher, he cultivated the habit of close observation and the congenial stance of scientific skepticism. He was privileged to work under professors with international reputations, almost all German imports and tough-

---

[2]*The Interpretation of Dreams* (1900), *SE* IV, 193.

minded positivists who disdained metaphysical speculations about, let alone pious explanations of, natural phenomena. Even after Freud modified their theories of the mind—in essence barely disguised physiological theories—he recalled his teachers with unfeigned gratitude. The most memorable of them, Ernst Brücke, an illustrious physiologist and a civilized but exacting taskmaster, confirmed Freud's bent as an unbeliever. Freud had grown up with no religious instruction at home, came to Vienna University as an atheist, and left it as an atheist—with persuasive scientific arguments.

In 1882, on Brücke's advice, Freud reluctantly left the laboratory to take a lowly post at the Vienna General Hospital. The reason was romantic: in April, he had met Martha Bernays, a slender, attractive young woman from northern Germany visiting one of his sisters, and fallen passionately in love. He was soon secretly engaged to her, but too poor to establish the respectable bourgeois household that he and his fiancée thought essential. It was not until September 1886, some five months after opening his practice in Vienna, with the aid of wedding gifts and loans from affluent friends, that the couple could marry. Within nine years, they had six children, the last of whom, Anna, grew up to be her father's confidante, secretary, nurse, disciple, and representative, and an eminent psychoanalyst in her own right.

Before his marriage, from October 1885 to February 1886, Freud worked in Paris with the celebrated French neurologist Jean-Martin Charcot, who impressed Freud with his bold advocacy of hypnosis as an instrument for healing medical disorders, and no less bold championship of the thesis (then quite unfashionable) that hysteria is an ailment to which men are susceptible no less than women. Charcot, an unrivaled observer, stimulated Freud's growing interest in the theoretical and therapeutic aspects of mental healing. Nervous ailments became Freud's specialty, and in the 1890s, as he told a friend, psychology became his tyrant. During these years he founded the psychoanalytic theory of mind.

He had intriguing if somewhat peculiar help. In 1887, he had met a nose-and-throat specialist from Berlin, Wilhelm Fliess, and rapidly established an intimate friendship with him. Fliess was the listener the lonely Freud craved: an intellectual gambler shocked at no idea, a propagator of provocative (at times fruitful) theories, an enthusiast who fed Freud ideas on which he could build. For over a decade, Fliess and Freud exchanged confidential letters and technical memoranda, meeting occasionally to explore their subversive notions. And Freud was propelled toward the discovery of psychoanalysis in his practice: his patients proved excellent teachers. He was increasingly specializing in women suffering from hysteria, and, observing their symptoms and listening to their complaints, he found that, though a good listener, he did not listen carefully enough. They had much to tell him.

In 1895, Freud and his fatherly friend Josef Breuer, a thriving, generous internist, published *Studies on Hysteria,* assigning Breuer's former patient "Anna O." pride of place. She had furnished fascinating material for intimate conversations between Breuer and Freud, and was to become, quite against her—and Breuer's—will, the founding patient of psychoanalysis. She demonstrated to Freud's satisfaction that hysteria originates in sexual malfunctioning and that symptoms can be talked away.

The year 1895 was decisive for Freud in other ways. In July, Freud managed to analyze a dream, his own, fully. He would employ this dream, known as "Irma's injection," as a model for psychoanalytic dream interpretation when he published it, some four years later, in his *Interpretation of*

Dreams. In the fall, he drafted, but neither completed nor published, what was later called the Project for a Scientific Psychology. It anticipated some of his fundamental theories yet serves as a reminder that Freud had been deeply enmeshed in the traditional physiological interpretation of mental events.

Increasingly Freud was offering psychological explanations for psychological phenomena. In the spring of 1896, he first used the fateful name, "psychoanalysis." Then in October his father died; "the most important event," he recalled a dozen years later, "the most poignant loss, of a man's life."[3] It supplied a powerful impetus toward psychoanalytic theorizing, stirring Freud to his unprecedented self-analysis, more systematic and thoroughgoing than the frankest autobiographer's self-probing. In the next three or four years, as he labored over his "Dream book," new discoveries crowded his days. But first he had to jettison the "seduction theory" he had championed for some time. It held that *every* neurosis results from premature sexual activity, mainly child molestation, in childhood.[4] Once freed from this far-reaching but improbable theory, Freud could appreciate the share of fantasies in mental life, and discover the Oedipus complex, that universal family triangle.

Freud's *Interpretation of Dreams* was published in November 1899.[5] It treated all dreams as wish fulfillments, detailed the mental stratagems that translate their causes into the strange drama the awakening dreamer remembers,

---

[3]Ibid., xxvi.

[4]Freud never claimed that sexual abuse does not exist. He had patients who he knew had not imagined the assaults they reported. All he abandoned when he abandoned the seduction theory was the sweeping claim that *only* the rape of a child, whether a boy or a girl, by a servant, an older sibling, or a classmate, could be the cause of a neurosis.

[5]The book bears the date of 1900 on the title page and this date is usually given as the date of publication.

and, in the difficult seventh chapter, outlined a comprehensive theory of mind. Its first reception was cool. During six years, only 351 copies were sold; a second edition did not appear until 1909. However, Freud's popularly written *Psychopathology of Everyday Life* of 1901 found a wider audience. Its collection of appealing slips of all sorts made Freud's fundamental point that the mind, however disheveled it might appear, is governed by firm rules. Thus—to give but one typical instance—the presiding officer of the Austrian parliament, facing a disagreeable season, opened it with the formal declaration that it was hereby closed. That "accident" had been prompted by his hidden repugnance for the sessions ahead.

Gradually, though still considered a radical, Freud acquired prestige and supporters. He had quarreled with Fliess in 1900, and, though their correspondence lingered on for some time, the two men never met again. Yet in 1902, after unconscionable delays, apparently generated by anti-Semitism combined with distrust of the maverick innovator, he was finally appointed an associate professor at the University of Vienna. Late that year, Freud and four other Viennese physicians began meeting every Wednesday night in his apartment at Berggasse 19 to discuss psychoanalytic questions; four years after, the group, grown to over a dozen regular participants, employed a paid secretary (Otto Rank) to take minutes and keep records. Finally, in 1908, it was transformed into the Vienna Psychoanalytic Society. At least some medical men (and a few women) were taking Freud's ideas seriously.

In 1905, Freud buttressed the structure of psychoanalytic thought with the second pillar of his theory: the *Three Essays on the Theory of Sexuality.* It outlined perversions and "normal" development from childhood to puberty with a lack of censoriousness and an openness hitherto virtually unknown in medical literature. Again in 1905, Freud brought out his book on jokes and the first of his famous case histories: "Fragment of an Analysis of a Case of Hysteria," nicknamed the "Dora case." He published it to illustrate the uses of dream interpretation in psychoanalysis, and expose his failure to recognize the power of transference in the analytic situation, but its lack of empathy with his embattled teen-age analysand has made it controversial.

In the following decade, Freud enriched the technique of psychoanalysis with three more sophisticated case histories—"Analysis of a Phobia in a Five-Year-Old Boy" ("Little Hans"), "Notes upon a Case of Obsessional Neurosis" ("Rat Man") in 1909, and "Psycho-Analytic Notes on an Autobiographical Account of a Case of Paranoia" ("Schreber Case") in 1911. Despite recent reanalyses, they remain lucid expository models across a wide spectrum of mental ailments. Then, from 1910 on, Freud published pioneering, exceedingly influential papers on technique, to establish psychoanalytic method on sound foundations. Nor did he neglect theory; witness such an important paper as "Formulations on the Two Principles of Mental Functioning" (1911), in which he differentiated between the "primary process," the primitive, unconscious element in the mind, and the "secondary process," largely conscious and controlled.

During these years, Freud also broke out of the circumscribed bounds of clinical and theoretical specialization by publishing papers on religion, literature, sexual mores, biography, sculpture, prehistory, and much else. "Obsessive Actions and Religious Practices" (1907), "Creative Writers and Daydreaming" (1908), " 'Civilized' Sexual Morality and Modern Nervous Illness" (1908), and his widely debated study of the origins of homosexuality, "Leonardo da Vinci and a Memory of His Childhood" (1910), are only samples of his range. Freud took all of culture as his province. He was realizing the program he had outlined for himself in his youth: to solve some of the great riddles of human existence.

Yet Freud also found the decade from 1905 to 1914 agitating with the progress of, and disagreeable splits within, a rapidly emerging international movement—*his* movement. Psychoanalytic politics took center stage. Two principal sources of hope for the future of Freud's ideas, and later of envenomed contention, were the intelligent, Socialist Viennese physician Alfred Adler (1870–1937), and the original, self-willed Swiss psychiatrist Carl G. Jung (1875–1961). Adler had been among Freud's earliest adherents and remained for some years his most prominent Viennese advocate. But as professional interest in psychoanalysis—not all of it benevolent—grew apace, as Freud's upsetting ideas were being explored at psychiatrists' congresses, Freud aspired to enlarge the reach of psychoanalysis beyond its place of origin. Vienna, with its handful of followers, struck him as provincial, unsuitable as headquarters.

The first breakthrough came in 1906, when Jung, then principal psychiatrist at the renowned clinic Burghölzli in Zurich, sent Freud an offprint. Freud responded promptly; a cordial correspondence blossomed, and the friendship was cemented by Jung's visit to Freud in early 1907. Freud was only fifty, vigorous and productive, but he had long brooded on himself as aging and decrepit. He was seeking a successor who would carry the psychoanalytic dispensation to later generations and into a world larger than the Viennese, Jewish ambiance to which psychoanalysis was then confined. Jung, a formidable presence and energetic debater, was an inspired discovery: he was not old, he was not Viennese, he was not Jewish. Jung was prominent in the first international congress of psychoanalysts at Salzburg in the spring of 1908, and was appointed, the following year, editor of a newly founded *Yearbook.* Freud, delighted with Jung, anointed him his son, his crown prince—accolades that Jung welcomed, indeed encouraged. Hence, when the International Psychoanalytic Association was founded in March 1910, in Nürnberg, Jung was Freud's logical, inevitable, choice for president. Freud's Viennese adherents saw their city displaced by Zurich as the center of psychoanalysis, and did not like it. A compromise was hammered out, and for some time peace reigned in the Vienna Psychoanalytic Society. But Adler was developing distinctive psychological ideas, which featured aggressiveness over sexuality, and "organ inferiority" as a dominant cause of neuroses. A split became inevitable, and, in the summer of 1911, Adler and some of his adherents resigned, leaving Freud and the Freudians in control of the Vienna society.

Freud was not without accolades. In September 1909, he had received an honorary doctorate at Clark University in Worcester, Massachusetts, as had Jung. But like Adler, Jung increasingly diverged from Freud's ideas. He had never been easy with the prominence Freud assigned to the sexual drive—libido. By early 1912, these reservations took a personal turn. In response, Ernest Jones, Freud's principal English lieutenant, formed a defensive secret band of like-minded analysts, the Committee. It consisted of himself, Freud, Sandor Ferenczi (a brilliant adherent from Budapest), the witty Viennese lawyer Hanns Sachs, the astute Berlin clinician and theorist Karl Abraham, and Freud's amanuensis, the autodidact Otto Rank. It seemed needed: by late 1912, the correspondence between Jung and Freud had grown acrimonious and in January 1914, Freud terminated his friendship with Jung. A split was only a matter of time; in the spring of 1914, Jung resigned from his powerful positions in the psychoanalytic movement.

The strains of psychoanalytic politics did not keep Freud

from continuing his explorations of an impressive variety of topics. In 1913, he published an audacious, highly speculative venture into psychoanalytic prehistory, *Totem and Taboo*, which specified the moment that savages, in some dim, remote past, entered culture by murdering their father and acquiring guilt feelings. Then, in 1914, he published (anonymously) "The Moses of Michelangelo," uniting his admiration for Michelangelo's brooding sculpture with his powers of observation. In the same year, with an unsettling paper on narcissism, he subverted crucial aspects of psychoanalytic thought by throwing doubts upon his theory of drives—hitherto divided into erotic and egoistic.

But harrowing events on the world stage shouldered aside Freud's reassessment of psychoanalytic theory. On June 28, 1914, Austria's Archduke Francis Ferdinand and his consort were assassinated. Six weeks later, on August 4, Europe was at war. The first casualty for psychoanalysis was Freud's eventually best-known case history, "From the History of an Infantile Neurosis" ("Wolf Man"), written in the fall of 1914, but not published until 1918. Psychoanalytic activity almost ground to a halt. Many potential patients were at the front; most psychoanalysts were drafted into the medical corps; communications between "enemies" like Ernest Jones and Freud were severely truncated; psychoanalytic publications almost vanished; and congresses, the lifeblood of communication, were out of the question. For Freud, these were anxious times in other ways: all three of his sons were in the army, two of them almost daily in mortal danger.

Yet the war did not idle Freud's mind. Having too much time on his hands, he used it to good purpose. Work was a defense against brooding. Between March and July 1915, he wrote a dozen fundamental papers on metapsychology—on the unconscious, on repression, on melancholia; but he refused to gather them into the basic textbook he had planned. He published five of the papers between 1915 and 1917, and destroyed the rest. His enigmatic dissatisfaction with them hints at the discontent that had fueled his paper on narcissism. His map of the mind was inadequate to the evidence he had accumulated in his clinical experience. But he still lacked a satisfactory alternative. That would have to wait until after the war.

Another wartime activity, though more successful, gave Freud only modest pleasure: beginning in 1915, he delivered lectures at the university, published as a single volume in 1917 as *Introductory Lectures on Psycho-Analysis.* With the cunning of the born popularizer, Freud opened with a series on ordinary experiences, slips of the tongue, "unmotivated" forgetting, then turned to dreams and concluded with the technical topic, neuroses. Frequently reprinted and widely translated, these *Introductory Lectures* finally secured Freud a wide audience.

The war dragged on. Originally, somewhat to his surprise, an Austrian patriot, Freud wearied of the endless slaughter. He grew appalled at the chauvinism of intellectuals, the callousness of commanders, the stupidity of politicians. He had not yet fully acknowledged the theoretical significance of aggression, even though psychoanalysts had regularly encountered aggressiveness among their patients. But the war, beastly as it was, confirmed the skeptical psychoanalytic appraisal of human nature.

Signs of revived activity came shortly before the end of hostilities. In September 1918, for the first time since 1913, psychoanalysts from Germany and Austria-Hungary met in Budapest. Two months later, the war was over. To the family's immense relief, all of Freud's sons survived it. But the time for worry was far from over. The defeated powers were faced with revolution, drastically transformed from empires into republics, and saddled with stringent, vindictive peace treaties stripping them of territory and resources. Vienna was hungry, cold, desperate; food and fuel shortages produced deadly ailments—tuberculosis and influenza. In this stressful situation, Freud, who wasted no tears on the departed Hapsburg Empire, proved an energetic, imaginative manager. The portrait of Martha Freud shielding Herr Professor from domestic realities needs revision. Freud dispatched precise requests abroad to relatives, friends, associates, specifying what nourishment and clothing his family needed most, and how to send packages safely. Then, in January 1920, postwar misery struck home with deadly force: Freud's beloved second daughter Sophie, married and living in Hamburg, mother of two children, died in the influenza epidemic.

It has been plausibly argued that her death suggested the pessimistic drive theory that Freud now developed. Actually, he had virtually completed *Beyond the Pleasure Principle* (1920), which first announced Freud's theory of the death drive, the year before. Once Freud had adopted this construct, in which the forces of life, Eros, dramatically confront the forces of death, Thanatos, he found himself unable to think any other way. In 1923, in his classic study *The Ego and the Id,* he completed his revisions. He now proposed a "structural theory" of the mind, which visualizes the mind as divided into three distinct yet interacting agencies: the id (the wholly unconscious domain of the mind, consisting of the drives and of material later repressed), the ego (which is partly conscious and contains the defense mechanisms and the capacities to calculate, reason, and plan), and the super-ego (also only partly conscious, which harbors the conscience and, beyond that, unconscious feelings of guilt). This new scheme did not lead Freud to abandon his classic characterization of mental activity—emphasizing the distance of thoughts from awareness—as either conscious, or preconscious, or wholly unconscious. But he now made the decisive point that many of the mental operations of the ego, and of the super-ego as well, are inaccessible to direct introspection.

Meanwhile, the psychoanalytic movement was flourishing. Freud was becoming a household word, though he detested the sensationalized attention the popular press gave him. Better: in 1920, at the first postwar congress at The Hague, former "enemies" met as friends. Freud was accompanied by his daughter Anna, whom he was then analyzing and who joined the Vienna Psychoanalytic Society in 1922. In that year, the analysts convened in Berlin. It was the last congress Freud ever attended. In April 1923, he was operated on for a growth in his palate. While for months his doctors and closest associates pretended that the growth was benign, by September the truth was out: he had cancer. Severe operations followed in the fall. From then on Freud, compelled to wear a prosthesis, was rarely free of discomfort or pain.

But he never stopped working. While he had trouble speaking, he continued to analyze patients, many of them American physicians who came to Vienna as his "pupils" and returned to analyze in New York or Chicago. He continued to revise his theories. From the mid-1920s on, he wrote controversial papers on female sexuality, and, in 1926, *Inhibitions, Symptoms, and Anxiety,* which reversed his earlier thinking on anxiety, now treating it as a danger signal. Moreover, he wrote essays that found a relatively wide public: *The Future of an Illusion,* a convinced atheist's dissection of religion, in 1927, and, in 1930, *Civilization and Its Discontents,* a disillusioned look at modern civilization on the verge of catastrophe.

In 1933, that catastrophe came. On January 30, Hitler was appointed chancellor in Germany, and from then on

Austrian Nazis, already active, increasingly intervened in politics. The old guard was disappearing: Karl Abraham had died prematurely in 1925; Sandor Ferenczi followed him in 1933. Freud's closest friends were gone. But Freud was unwilling to leave the Vienna he hated and loved: he was too old, he did not want to desert, and besides, the Nazis would never invade his country. On the morning of March 12, 1938, the Germans proved him wrong. As the Nazis marched in, a jubilant populace greeted them. Spontaneous anti-Semitic outrages surpassed anything Germans had witnessed after five years of Nazi rule. Late in March, Anna was summoned to Gestapo headquarters; while she was released unharmed, the trauma changed Freud's mind: he must emigrate. It took months to satisfy the Nazi government's extortions, but on June 4, Freud left for Paris, welcomed by his former analysand and loving disciple, Princess Marie Bonaparte. On June 6, Freud landed in London, preceded by most of his family, "to die in freedom."

Aged and ill, he kept on working. Freud's last completed book, *Moses and Monotheism,* irritated and dismayed his Jewish readers with its assertion that Moses had been an Egyptian: he ended life as he had lived it—a disturber of the peace. He died bravely on September 23, 1939, asking his physician for a lethal dose of morphine. Freud did not believe in personal immortality, but his work lives on.

ABOUT THIS BOOK

In 1909, Clark University at Worcester, Massachusetts, presided over by the ambitious and imaginative psychologist G. Stanley Hall, celebrated the twentieth anniversary of its founding with a series of conferences and lectures. One of its visiting eminences was Sigmund Freud, invited to give five lectures on his new psychology and accept an honorary degree. Late in August, accompanied by his young Hungarian adherent Sandor Ferenczi and C. G. Jung (who was also to lecture and receive an honorary degree) Freud took ship to the United States, for his only visit. The American trip is awash with irony: the honorary degree that Clark bestowed on Freud was the first, and for many years the only, official recognition he would receive, yet Freud's conventional and articulate disdain for materialistic and uncultivated America never abated.

Freud lectured on the foundations of psychoanalysis, including its scandalous candor about sexuality, to attentive and respectful audiences—in German. He improvised each of these addresses: in the morning, Freud would take a walk with Ferenczi, discuss with him the topic of the day, and then speak without notes. Upon his return to Vienna, he reconstructed his five American lectures from memory, apparently quite accurately. *Über Psychoanalyse* was published in 1910, and translated the same year as "The Origin and Development of Psychoanalysis." Until the far more extensive *Introductory Lectures on Psycho-Analysis* (1917), *Five Lectures on Psycho-Analysis* was the authoritative summary of Freud's ideas. It was well received and remains a lucid general introduction to what is, after all, a difficult discipline.

EDITOR'S NOTE

Über Psychoanalyse

(a) GERMAN EDITIONS:

1910 Leipzig and Vienna: Deuticke. Pp. 62. (2nd ed. 1912, 3rd ed. 1916, 4th ed. 1919, 5th ed. 1920, 6th ed. 1922, 7th ed. 1924, 8th ed. 1930; all unchanged.)

1924 G.S., 4, 349–406. (Slightly changed.)

1943 G.W., 8, 3-60. (Unchanged from G.S.)

(b) ENGLISH TRANSLATION:

'The Origin and Development of Psychoanalysis'

1910 Am. J. Psychol., 21 (2 and 3), 181–218. (Tr. H. W. Chase.)

1910 In Lectures and Addresses Delivered before the Departments of Psychology and Pedagogy in Celebration of the Twentieth Anniversary of the Opening of Clark University, Worcester, Mass., Part I, pp. 1–38. (Reprint of above.)

1924 In An Outline of Psychoanalysis, ed. Van Teslaar, New York: Boni and Liveright. Pp. 21–70. (Reissue of above.)

The present, entirely new translation, with the different title Five Lectures on Psycho-Analysis, is by James Strachey.

In 1909, Clark University, Worcester, Massachusetts, celebrated the twentieth year of its foundation, and its President, Dr. G. Stanley Hall, invited Freud and some of his principal followers (C. G. Jung, S. Ferenczi, Ernest Jones, and A. A. Brill) to take part in the occasion and to be awarded honorary degrees. It was in December, 1908, that Freud first received the invitation, but it was not until the following autumn that the event took place, and Freud's five lectures were delivered on Monday, September 6, 1909, and the four following days. This, as Freud himself declared at the time, was the first official recognition of the young science, and he has described in his *Autobiographical Study* (1925*d*, Chapter V) how, as he stepped on to the platform to deliver his lectures, 'it seemed like the realization of some incredible day-dream'.[1]

The lectures (in German, of course) were, according to Freud's almost universal practice, delivered extempore and, as we learn from Dr. Jones, without notes and after very little preparation. It was only after his return to Vienna that he was induced unwillingly to write them out. This work was not finished till the second week of December, but his verbal memory was so good that, as Dr. Jones assures us, the printed version 'did not depart much from the original delivery'. Their first publication was in an English translation in the *American Journal of Psychology* early in 1910, but the original German appeared soon afterwards as a pamphlet in Vienna.[2] The work proved a popular one and it passed

---

[1]Another account of the occasion will be found in the 'History of the Psycho-Analytic Movement' (1914*d*). A fuller description, from which most of the details given here are derived, is contained in Ernest Jones's biography (1955, 59 ff.).

[2]During Freud's lifetime the lectures were translated into many other languages: Polish (1911), Russian (1911), Hungarian (1912), Dutch (1912), Italian (1915), Danish (1920), French (1921), Spanish (1923), Portuguese (1931), and Japanese (1933).

through several editions; in none of these, however, was any alteration of substance made, except for the footnote added in 1923 at the very beginning, and appearing in the *Gesammelte Schriften* and *Gesammelte Werke* only, in which Freud retracted his expressions of indebtedness to Breuer. Some discussion of Freud's varying attitude to Breuer will be found in the Editor's Introduction to *Studies on Hysteria, Standard Ed.,* 2, xxvi ff.

All through his career Freud was constantly ready to give expositions of his discoveries. (A list of these will be found below, on pp. 63–64.) He had already published some short accounts of psycho-analysis, but this set of lectures was the first on an extended scale. These expositions naturally varied in difficulty according to the audience for which they were designed, and this must be reckoned among the simplest ones, especially when compared with the great series of *Introductory Lectures* delivered a few years later (1916–17). Nevertheless, in spite of all the additions that were to be made to the structure of psycho-analysis during the following quarter of a century, these lectures still provide an admirable preliminary picture which calls for very little correction. And they give an excellent idea of the ease and clarity of style and the unconstrained sense of form which made Freud such a remarkable expository lecturer.

Considerable extracts from the earlier (1910) translation of this work were included in Rickman's *General Selection from the Works of Sigmund Freud* (1937, 3-43).

FIVE LECTURES
ON
PSYCHO-ANALYSIS

First Lecture

Ladies and Gentlemen,—It is with novel and bewildering feelings that I find myself in the New World, lecturing before an audience of expectant enquirers. No doubt I owe this honour only to the fact that my name is linked with the topic of psycho-analysis; and it is of psycho-analysis, therefore, that I intend to speak to you. I shall attempt to give you, as succinctly as possible, a survey of the history and subsequent development of this new method of examination and treatment.

If it is a merit to have brought psycho-analysis into being, that merit is not mine.[1] I had no share in its earliest beginnings. I was a student and working for my final examinations at the time when another Viennese physician, Dr. Josef Breuer,[2] first (in 1880–2) made use of this procedure on a girl who was suffering from hysteria. Let us turn our atten-

---

[1](*Footnote added* 1923:) See, however, in this connection my remarks in 'A History of the Psycho-Analytic Movement' (1914*d*), where I assumed the entire responsibility for psycho-analysis.

[2]Dr. Josef Breuer, born in 1842, a Corresponding Member of the Kaiserliche Akademie der Wissenschaften [Imperial Academy of Sciences], is well known for his work on respiration and on the physiology of the sense of equilibrium. [His obituary by Freud (1925*g*) included a more detailed account of his career.]

tion straightaway to the history of this case and its treatment, which you will find set out in detail in the *Studies on Hysteria* [1895*d*]³ which were published later by Breuer and myself.

But I should like to make one preliminary remark. It is not without satisfaction that I have learnt that the majority of my audience are not members of the medical profession. You have no need to be afraid that any special medical knowledge will be required for following what I have to say. It is true that we shall go along with the doctors on the first stage of our journey, but we shall soon part company with them and, with Dr. Breuer, shall pursue a quite individual path.

Dr. Breuer's patient was a girl of twenty-one, of high intellectual gifts. Her illness lasted for over two years, and in the course of it she developed a series of physical and psychological disturbances which decidedly deserved to be taken seriously. She suffered from a rigid paralysis, accompanied by loss of sensation, of both extremities on the right side of her body; and the same trouble from time to time affected her on her left side. Her eye movements were disturbed and her power of vision was subject to numerous restrictions. She had difficulties over the posture of her head; she had a severe nervous cough. She had an aversion to taking nourishment, and on one occasion she was for several weeks unable to drink in spite of a tormenting thirst. Her powers of speech were reduced, even to the point of her

---

³Some of my contributions to this book have been translated into English by Dr. A. A. Brill of New York: *Selected Papers on Hysteria* (New York, 1909). [This was the first Freud book to appear in English. The complete Breuer and Freud *Studies* were translated by Brill later (New York, 1936). A new translation appeared in 1955, forming the second volume of the Freud *Standard Edition*, where the case history of this patient (Fräulein Anna O.) will be found on p. 21 ff.]

being unable to speak or understand her native language. Finally, she was subject to conditions of *'absence'*, [4] of confusion, of delirium, and of alteration of her whole personality, to which we shall have presently to turn our attention.

When you hear such an enumeration of symptoms, you will be inclined to think it safe to assume, even though you are not doctors, that what we have before us is a severe illness, probably affecting the brain, that it offers small prospect of recovery and will probably lead to the patient's early decease. You must be prepared to learn from the doctors, however, that, in a number of cases which display severe symptoms such as these, it is justifiable to take a different and a far more favourable view. If a picture of this kind is presented by a young patient of the female sex, whose vital internal organs (heart, kidneys, etc.) are shown on objective examination to be normal, but who has been subjected to violent *emotional* shocks—if, moreover, her various symptoms differ in certain matters of detail from what would have been expected—then doctors are not inclined to take the case too seriously. They decide that what they have before them is not an organic disease of the brain, but the enigmatic condition which, from the time of ancient Greek medicine, has been known as 'hysteria' and which has the power of producing illusory pictures of a whole number of serious diseases. They consider that there is then no risk to life but that a return to health—even a complete one—is probable. It is not always quite easy to distinguish a hysteria like this from a severe organic illness. There is no need for us to know, however, how a differential diagnosis of that kind is made; it will suffice to have an assurance that the case of Breuer's patient was precisely of a kind in which no competent physician could fail to make a diagnosis of hys-

---

[4] [The French term.]

teria. And here we may quote from the report of the patient's illness the further fact that it made its appearance at a time when she was nursing her father, of whom she was devotedly fond, through the grave illness which led to his death, and that, as a result of her own illness, she was obliged to give up nursing him.

So far it has been an advantage to us to accompany the doctors; but the moment of parting is at hand. For you must not suppose that a patient's prospects of medical assistance are improved in essentials by the fact that a diagnosis of hysteria has been substituted for one of severe organic disease of the brain. Medical skill is in most cases powerless against severe diseases of the brain; but neither can the doctor do anything against hysterical disorders. He must leave it to kindly Nature to decide when and how his optimistic prognosis shall be fulfilled.[5]

Thus the recognition of the illness as hysteria makes little difference to the patient; but to the doctor quite the reverse. It is noticeable that his attitude towards hysterical patients is quite other than towards sufferers from organic diseases. He does not have the same sympathy for the former as for the latter: for the hysteric's ailment is in fact far less serious and yet it seems to claim to be regarded as equally so. And there is a further factor at work. Through his studies, the doctor has learnt many things that remain a sealed book to the layman: he has been able to form ideas on the causes of illness and on the changes it brings about—e.g. in the brain of a person suffering from apoplexy or from a malignant growth—ideas which must to some degree meet the case, since they allow him to understand the details of the illness.

---

[5] I am aware that this is no longer the case; but in my lecture I am putting myself and my hearers back into the period before 1880. If things are different now, that is to a great extent the result of the activities whose history I am now sketching.

But all his knowledge—his training in anatomy, in physiology and in pathology—leaves him in the lurch when he is confronted by the details of hysterical phenomena. He cannot understand hysteria, and in the face of it he is himself a layman. This is not a pleasant situation for anyone who as a rule sets so much store by his knowledge. So it comes about that hysterical patients forfeit his sympathy. He regards them as people who are transgressing the laws of his science—like heretics in the eyes of the orthodox. He attributes every kind of wickedness to them, accuses them of exaggeration, of deliberate deceit, of malingering. And he punishes them by withdrawing his interest from them.

Dr. Breuer's attitude towards his patient deserved no such reproach. He gave her both sympathy and interest, even though, to begin with, he did not know how to help her. It seems likely that she herself made his task easier by the admirable qualities of intellect and character to which he has testified in her case history. Soon, moreover, his benevolent scrutiny showed him the means of bringing her a first instalment of help.

It was observed that, while the patient was in her states of *'absence'* (altered personality accompanied by confusion), she was in the habit of muttering a few words to herself which seemed as though they arose from some train of thought that was occupying her mind. The doctor, after getting a report of these words, used to put her into a kind of hypnosis and then repeat them to her so as to induce her to use them as a starting-point. The patient complied with the plan, and in this way reproduced in his presence the mental creations which had been occupying her mind during the *'absences'* and which had betrayed their existence by the fragmentary words which she had uttered. They were profoundly melancholy phantasies—'day-dreams' we should call them—sometimes characterized by poetic beauty, and their starting-point was as a rule the position of a girl at her father's sick-bed. When she had related a number of these phantasies, she was as if set free, and she was brought back to normal mental life. The improvement in her condition, which would last for several hours, would be succeeded next day by a further attack of *'absence'*; and this in turn would be removed in the same way by getting her to put into words her freshly constructed phantasies. It was impossible to escape the conclusion that the alteration in her mental state which was expressed in the *'absences'* was a result of the stimulus proceeding from these highly emotional phantasies. The patient herself, who, strange to say, could at this time only speak and understand English, christened this novel kind of treatment the 'talking cure'[6] or used to refer to it jokingly as 'chimney-sweeping'.[6]

It soon emerged, as though by chance, that this process of sweeping the mind clean could accomplish more than the merely temporary relief of her ever-recurring mental confusion. It was actually possible to bring about the disappearance of the painful symptoms of her illness, if she could be brought to remember under hypnosis, with an accompanying expression of affect, on what occasion and in what connection the symptoms had first appeared. 'It was in the summer during a period of extreme heat, and the patient was suffering very badly from thirst; for, without being able to account for it in any way, she suddenly found it impossible to drink. She would take up the glass of water that she longed for, but as soon as it touched her lips she would push it away like someone suffering from hydrophobia. As she did this, she was obviously in an *absence* for a couple of seconds. She lived only on fruit, such as melons, etc., so as to lessen her tormenting thirst. This had lasted for some six weeks,

---

[6][These phrases are in English in the original.]

when one day during hypnosis she grumbled about her English "lady-companion", whom she did not care for, and went on to describe, with every sign of disgust, how she had once gone into this lady's room and how her little dog—horrid creature!—had drunk out of a glass there. The patient had said nothing, as she had wanted to be polite. After giving further energetic expression to the anger she had held back, she asked for something to drink, drank a large quantity of water without any difficulty, and awoke from her hypnosis with the glass at her lips; and thereupon the disturbance vanished, never to return.'[7]

With your permission, I should like to pause a moment over this event. Never before had anyone removed a hysterical symptom by such a method or had thus gained so deep an insight into its causation. It could not fail to prove a momentous discovery if the expectation were confirmed that others of the patient's symptoms—perhaps the majority of them—had arisen and could be removed in this same manner. Breuer spared no pains in convincing himself that this was so, and he proceeded to a systematic investigation of the pathogenesis of the other and more serious symptoms of the patient's illness. And it really *was* so. Almost all the symptoms had arisen in this way as residues—'precipitates' they might be called—of emotional experiences. To these experiences, therefore, we later gave the name of 'psychical traumas', while the particular nature of the symptoms was explained by their relation to the traumatic scenes which were their cause. They were, to use a technical term, 'determined' by the scenes of whose recollection they represented residues, and it was no longer necessary to describe them as capricious or enigmatic products of the neurosis. One unexpected point, however, must be noticed. What left the

---

[7] *Studies on Hysteria* [*Standard Ed.*, **2**, 34].

symptom behind was not always a *single* experience. On the
contrary, the result was usually brought about by the conver-
gence of several traumas, and often by the repetition of a
great number of similar ones. Thus it was necessary to repro-
duce the whole chain of pathogenic memories in chronologi-
cal order, or rather in reversed order, the latest ones first and
the earliest ones last; and it was quite impossible to jump
over the later traumas in order to get back more quickly to
the first, which was often the most potent one.

No doubt you will now ask me for some further instances
of the causation of hysterical symptoms besides the one I
have already given you of a fear of water produced by disgust
at a dog drinking out of a glass. But if I am to keep to my
programme I shall have to restrict myself to very few examples. In regard to the patient's disturbances of vision, for
instance, Breuer describes how they were traced back to
occasions such as one on which, 'when she was sitting by her
father's bedside with tears in her eyes, he suddenly asked her
what time it was. She could not see clearly; she made a great
effort, and brought her watch near to her eyes. The face of
the watch now seemed very big—thus accounting for her
macropsia and convergent squint. Or again, she tried hard
to suppress her tears so that the sick man should not see
them.'[8] Moreover, all of the pathogenic impressions came
from the period during which she was helping to nurse her
sick father. 'She once woke up during the night in great
anxiety about the patient, who was in a high fever; and she
was under the strain of expecting the arrival of a surgeon
from Vienna who was to operate. Her mother had gone
away for a short time and Anna was sitting at the bedside
with her right arm over the back of her chair. She fell into
a waking dream and saw a black snake coming towards the

------

[8]*Studies on Hysteria* [Standard Ed., 2, 39–40].

sick man from the wall to bite him. (It is most likely that there were in fact snakes in the field behind the house and that these had previously given the girl a fright; they would thus have provided the material for her hallucination.) She tried to keep the snake off, but it was as though she was paralysed. Her right arm, over the back of the chair, had gone to sleep, and had become anaesthetic and paretic; and when she looked at it the fingers turned into little snakes with death's heads (the nails). (It seems probable that she had tried to use her paralysed right hand to drive off the snake and that its anaesthesia and paralysis had consequently become associated with the hallucination of the snake.) When the snake vanished, in her terror she tried to pray. But language failed her: she could find no tongue in which to speak, till at last she thought of some children's verses in English and then found herself able to think and pray in that language.'[9] When the patient had recollected this scene in hypnosis, the rigid paralysis of her left arm, which had persisted since the beginning of her illness, disappeared, and the treatment was brought to an end.

When, some years later, I began to employ Breuer's method of examination and treatment on patients of my own, my experiences agreed entirely with his. A lady, aged about forty, suffered from a *tic* consisting of a peculiar 'clacking' sound which she produced whenever she was excited, or sometimes for no visible reason. It had its origin in two experiences, whose common element lay in the fact that at the moment of their occurrence she had formed a determination not to make any noise, and in the fact that on both these occasions a kind of counter-will led her to break the silence with this same sound. On the first of these occasions one of her children had been ill, and, when she had at last

---

[9]*Studies on Hysteria* [*Standard Ed.*, 2, 38–9].

with great difficulty succeeded in getting it off to sleep, she had said to herself that she must keep absolutely still so as not to wake it. On the other occasion, while she was driving with her two children in a thunderstorm, the horses had bolted and she had carefully tried to avoid making any noise for fear of frightening them even more.[10] I give you this one example out of a number of others which are reported in the *Studies on Hysteria.* [11]

Ladies and Gentlemen, if I may be allowed to generalize—which is unavoidable in so condensed an account as this—I should like to formulate what we have learned so far as follows: *our hysterical patients suffer from reminiscences.* Their symptoms are residues and mnemic symbols of particular (traumatic) experiences. We may perhaps obtain a deeper understanding of this kind of symbolism if we compare them with other mnemic symbols in other fields. The monuments and memorials with which large cities are adorned are also mnemic symbols. If you take a walk through the streets of London, you will find, in front of one of the great railway termini, a richly carved Gothic column— Charing Cross. One of the old Plantagenet kings of the thirteenth century ordered the body of his beloved Queen Eleanor to be carried to Westminster; and at every stage at which the coffin rested he erected a Gothic cross. Charing Cross is the last of the monuments that commemorate the

---

[10]*Studies on Hysteria* [*Standard Ed.,* **2,** 54 and 58].
[11]Extracts from that volume, together with some later writings of mine on hysteria, are now to be had in an English translation prepared by Dr. A. A. Brill of New York. [See footnote p. 4. The case here reported is that of Frau Emmy von N., the second in *Studies on Hysteria, Standard Ed.,* **2,** 48 ff.]

funeral cortège.[12] At another point in the same town, not far from London Bridge, you will find a towering, and more modern, column, which is simply known as 'The Monument'. It was designed as a memorial of the Great Fire, which broke out in that neighbourhood in 1666 and destroyed a large part of the city. These monuments, then, resemble hysterical symptoms in being mnemic symbols; up to that point the comparison seems justifiable. But what should we think of a Londoner who paused to-day in deep melancholy before the memorial of Queen Eleanor's funeral instead of going about his business in the hurry that modern working conditions demand or instead of feeling joy over the youthful queen of his own heart? Or again what should we think of a Londoner who shed tears before the Monument that commemorates the reduction of his beloved metropolis to ashes although it has long since risen again in far greater brilliance? Yet every single hysteric and neurotic behaves like these two unpractical Londoners. Not only do they remember painful experiences of the remote past, but they still cling to them emotionally; they cannot get free of the past and for its sake they neglect what is real and immediate. This fixation of mental life to pathogenic traumas is one of the most significant and practically important characteristics of neurosis.

I am quite ready to allow the justice of an objection that you are probably raising at this moment on the basis of the case history of Breuer's patient. It is quite true that all her traumas dated from the period when she was nursing her sick father and that her symptoms can only be regarded as

---

[12]Or rather, it is a modern copy of one of these monuments. As Dr. Ernest Jones tells me, the name 'Charing' is believed to be derived from the words *'chère reine'*.

mnemic signs of his illness and death. Thus they correspond to a display of mourning, and there is certainly nothing pathological in being fixated to the memory of a dead person so short a time after his decease; on the contrary, it would be a normal emotional process. I grant you that in the case of Breuer's patient there is nothing striking in her fixation to her trauma. But in other cases—such as that of the *tic* that I treated myself, where the determinants dated back more than fifteen and ten years—the feature of an abnormal attachment to the past is very clear; and it seems likely that Breuer's patient would have developed a similar feature if she had not received cathartic treatment so soon after experiencing the traumas and developing the symptoms.

So far we have only been discussing the relations between a patient's hysterical symptoms and the events of her life. There are, however, two further factors in Breuer's observation which enable us to form some notion of how the processes of falling ill and of recovering occur.

In the first place, it must be emphasized that Breuer's patient, in almost all her pathogenic situations, was obliged to *suppress* a powerful emotion instead of allowing its discharge in the appropriate signs of emotion, words or actions. In the episode of her lady-companion's dog, she suppressed any manifestation of her very intense disgust, out of consideration for the woman's feelings; while she watched at her father's bedside she was constantly on the alert to prevent the sick man from observing her anxiety and her painful depression. When subsequently she reproduced these scenes in her doctor's presence the affect which had been inhibited at the time emerged with peculiar violence, as though it had been saved up for a long time. Indeed, the symptom which was left over from one of these scenes would reach its highest pitch of intensity at the time when its determining cause was being approached, only to vanish when that cause had been fully ventilated. On the other hand, it was found that no result was produced by the recollection of a scene in the doctor's presence if for some reason the recollection took place without any generation of affect. Thus it was what happened to these affects, which might be regarded as displaceable magnitudes, that was the decisive factor both for the onset of illness and for recovery. One was driven to assume that the illness occurred because the affects generated in the pathogenic situations had their normal outlet blocked, and that the essence of the illness lay in the fact that these 'strangulated' affects were then put to an abnormal use. In part they remained as a permanent burden upon the patient's mental life and a source of constant excitation for it; and in part they underwent a transformation into unusual somatic innervations and inhibitions, which manifested themselves as the physical symptoms of the case. For this latter process we coined the term 'hysterical conversion'. Quite apart from this, a certain portion of our mental excitation is normally directed along the paths of somatic innervation and produces what we know as an 'expression of the emotions'. Hysterical conversion exaggerates this portion of the discharge of an emotionally cathected mental process; it represents a far more intense expression of the emotions, which has entered upon a new path. When the bed of a stream is divided into two channels, then, if the current in one of them is brought up against an obstacle, the other will at once be overfilled. As you see, we are on the point of arriving at a purely psychological theory of hysteria, with affective processes in the front rank.

A second observation of Breuer's, again, compels us to attach great importance, among the characteristics of the pathological chain of events, to states of consciousness. Breuer's patient exhibited, alongside of her normal state, a

number of mental peculiarities: conditions of *'absence'*, confusion, and alterations of character. In her normal state she
knew nothing of the pathogenic scenes or their connection
with her symptoms; she had forgotten the scenes, or at all
events had severed the pathogenic link. When she was put
under hypnosis, it was possible, at the expense of a considerable amount of labour, to recall the scenes to her memory;
and, through this work of recollecting, the symptoms were
removed. The explanation of this fact would be a most
awkward business, were it not that the way is pointed by
experiences and experiments in hypnotism. The study of
hypnotic phenomena has accustomed us to what was at first
a bewildering realization that in one and the same individual
there can be several mental groupings, which can remain
more or less independent of one another, which can 'know
nothing' of one another and which can alternate with one
another in their hold upon consciousness. Cases of this kind,
too, occasionally appear spontaneously, and are then described as examples of *'double conscience'*. [13] If, where a
splitting of the personality such as this has occurred, consciousness remains attached regularly to one of the two
states, we call it the *conscious* mental state and the other,
which is detached from it, the *unconscious* one. In the
familiar condition known as 'post-hypnotic suggestion', a
command given under hypnosis is slavishly carried out
subsequently in the normal state. This phenomenon affords
an admirable example of the influences which the unconscious state can exercise over the conscious one; moreover,
it provides a pattern upon which we can account for the
phenomena of hysteria. Breuer adopted a hypothesis that
hysterical symptoms arise in peculiar mental conditions to
which he gave the name of 'hypnoid'. On this view, excita-

---

[13][The French term for 'dual consciousness'.]

tions occurring during these hypnoid states can easily become pathogenic because such states do not provide opportunities for the normal discharge of the process of excitation. There consequently arises from the process of excitation an unusual product—the symptom. This finds its way, like a foreign body, into the normal state, which in turn is in ignorance of the hypnoid pathogenic situation. Wherever there is a symptom there is also an amnesia, a gap in the memory, and filling up this gap implies the removal of the conditions which led to the production of the symptom.

This last part of my account will not, I fear, strike you as particularly clear. But you should bear in mind that we are dealing with novel and difficult considerations, and it may well be that it is not possible to make them much clearer—which shows that we still have a long way to go in our knowledge of the subject. Moreover, Breuer's theory of 'hypnoid states' turned out to be impeding and unnecessary, and it has been dropped by psycho-analysis to-day. Later on, you will at least have a hint of the influences and processes that were to be discovered behind the screen of hypnoid states erected by Breuer. You will have rightly formed the opinion, too, that Breuer's investigation has only succeeded in offering you a very incomplete theory and an unsatisfying explanation of the phenomena observed. But complete theories do not fall ready-made from the sky and you would have even better grounds for suspicion if anyone presented you with a flawless and complete theory at the very beginning of his observations. Such a theory could only be a child of his speculation and could not be the fruit of an unprejudiced examination of the facts.

Second Lecture

Ladies and Gentlemen,—At about the same time at which Breuer was carrying on the 'talking cure' with his patient, the great Charcot in Paris had begun the researches into hysterical patients at the Salpêtrière which were to lead to a new understanding of the disease. There was no possibility of his findings being known in Vienna at that time. But when, some ten years later, Breuer and I published our 'Preliminary Communication' on the psychical mechanism of hysterical phenomena [1893a], we were completely under the spell of Charcot's researches. We regarded the pathogenic experiences of our patients as psychical traumas, and equated them with the somatic traumas whose influence on hysterical paralyses had been established by Charcot; and Breuer's hypothesis of hypnoid states was itself nothing but a reflection of the fact that Charcot had reproduced those traumatic paralyses artificially under hypnosis.

The great French observer, whose pupil I became in 1885–6, was not himself inclined to adopt a psychological outlook. It was his pupil, Pierre Janet, who first attempted a deeper approach to the peculiar psychical processes present in hysteria, and we followed his example when we took the splitting of the mind and dissociation of the personality as the centre of our position. You will find in Janet a theory of hysteria which takes into account the prevailing views in France on the part played by heredity and degeneracy. According to him, hysteria is a form of degenerate modification of the nervous system, which shows itself in an innate weakness in the power of psychical synthesis. Hysterical patients, he believes, are inherently incapable of holding together the multiplicity of mental processes into a unity, and hence arises the tendency to mental dissociation. If I may be allowed to draw a homely but clear analogy, Janet's hysterical patient reminds one of a feeble woman who has gone out shopping and is now returning home laden with a multitude of parcels and boxes. She cannot contain the whole heap of them with her two arms and ten fingers. So first of all one object slips from her grasp; and when she stoops to pick it up, another one escapes her in its place, and so on. This supposed mental weakness of hysterical patients is not confirmed when we find that, alongside these phenomena of diminished capacity, examples are also to be observed of a partial increase in efficiency, as though by way of compensation. At the time when Breuer's patient had forgotten her mother tongue and every other language but English, her grasp of English reached such heights that, if she was handed a German book, she was able straight away to read out a correct and fluent translation of it.

When, later on, I set about continuing on my own account the investigations that had been begun by Breuer, I soon arrived at another view of the origin of hysterical dissociation (the splitting of consciousness). A divergence of this kind, which was to be decisive for everything that followed, was inevitable, since I did not start out, like Janet, from laboratory experiments, but with therapeutic aims in mind.

I was driven forward above all by practical necessity. The cathartic procedure, as carried out by Breuer, presupposed putting the patient into a state of deep hypnosis; for it was only in a state of hypnosis that he attained a knowledge of the pathogenic connections which escaped him in his normal state. But I soon came to dislike hypnosis, for it was a temperamental and, one might almost say, a mystical ally. When I found that, in spite of all my efforts, I could not succeed in bringing more than a fraction of my patients into a hypnotic state, I determined to give up hypnosis and to make the cathartic procedure independent of it. Since I was not able at will to alter the mental state of the majority of my patients, I set about working with them in their *normal* state. At first, I must confess, this seemed a senseless and hopeless undertaking. I was set the task of learning from the patient something that I did not know and that he did not know himself. How could one hope to elicit it? But there came to my help a recollection of a most remarkable and instructive experiment which I had witnessed when I was with Bernheim at Nancy [in 1889]. Bernheim showed us that people whom he had put into a state of hypnotic somnambulism, and who had had all kinds of experiences while they were in that state, only *appeared* to have lost the memory of what they had experienced during somnambulism; it was possible to revive these memories in their normal state. It is true that, when he questioned them about their somnambulistic experiences, they began by maintaining that they knew nothing about them; but if he refused to give way, and insisted, and assured them that they *did* know about them, the forgotten experiences always reappeared.

So I did the same thing with my patients. When I reached a point with them at which they maintained that they knew nothing more, I assured them that they *did* know it all the same, and that they had only to say it; and I ventured to declare that the right memory would occur to them at the moment at which I laid my hand on their forehead. In that way I succeeded, without using hypnosis, in obtaining from the patients whatever was required for establishing the connection between the pathogenic scenes they had forgotten and the symptoms left over from those scenes. But it was a laborious procedure, and in the long run an exhausting one; and it was unsuited to serve as a permanent technique.

I did not abandon it, however, before the observations I made during my use of it afforded me decisive evidence. I found confirmation of the fact that the forgotten memories were not lost. They were in the patient's possession and were ready to emerge in association to what was still known by him; but there was some force that prevented them from becoming conscious and compelled them to remain unconscious. The existence of this force could be assumed with certainty, since one became aware of an effort corresponding to it if, in opposition to it, one tried to introduce the unconscious memories into the patient's consciousness. The force which was maintaining the pathological condition became apparent in the form of *resistance* on the part of the patient.

It was on this idea of resistance, then, that I based my view of the course of psychical events in hysteria. In order to effect a recovery, it had proved necessary to remove these resistances. Starting out from the mechanism of cure, it now became possible to construct quite definite ideas of the origin of the illness. The same forces which, in the form of resistance, were now offering opposition to the forgotten material's being made conscious, must formerly have brought about the forgetting and must have pushed the pathogenic experiences in question out of consciousness. I gave the name of *'repression'* to this hypothetical process, and I considered that it was proved by the undeniable existence of resistance.

The further question could then be raised as to what these forces were and what the determinants were of the repression in which we now recognized the pathogenic mechanism of hysteria. A comparative study of the pathogenic situations which we had come to know through the cathartic procedure made it possible to answer this question. All these experiences had involved the emergence of a wishful impulse which was in sharp contrast to the subject's other wishes and which proved incompatible with the ethical and aesthetic standards of his personality. There had been a short conflict, and the end of this internal struggle was that the idea which had appeared before consciousness as the vehicle of this irreconcilable wish fell a victim to repression, was pushed out of consciousness with all its attached memories, and was forgotten. Thus the incompatibility of the wish in question with the patient's ego was the motive for the repression; the subject's ethical and other standards were the repressing forces. An acceptance of the incompatible wishful impulse or a prolongation of the conflict would have produced a high degree of unpleasure; this unpleasure was avoided by means of repression, which was thus revealed as one of the devices serving to protect the mental personality.

To take the place of a number of instances, I will relate a single one of my cases, in which the determinants and advantages of repression are sufficiently evident. For my present purpose I shall have once again to abridge the case history and omit some important underlying material. The patient was a girl,[1] who had lost her beloved father after she had taken a share in nursing him—a situation analogous to that of Breuer's patient. Soon afterwards her elder sister married, and her new brother-in-law aroused in her a pecu-

---

[1][This is the case of Fräulein Elisabeth von R., the fifth of the case histories fully reported in *Studies on Hysteria, Standard Ed.*, 2, 135 ff.]

liar feeling of sympathy which was easily masked under a disguise of family affection. Not long afterwards her sister fell ill and died, in the absence of the patient and her mother. They were summoned in all haste without being given any definite information of the tragic event. When the girl reached the bedside of her dead sister, there came to her for a brief moment an idea that might be expressed in these words: 'Now he is free and can marry me.' We may assume with certainty that this idea, which betrayed to her consciousness the intense love for her brother-in-law of which she had not herself been conscious, was surrendered to repression a moment later, owing to the revolt of her feelings. The girl fell ill with severe hysterical symptoms; and while she was under my treatment it turned out that she had completely forgotten the scene by her sister's bedside and the odious egoistic impulse that had emerged in her. She remembered it during the treatment and reproduced the pathogenic moment with signs of the most violent emotion, and, as a result of the treatment, she became healthy once more.

Perhaps I may give you a more vivid picture of repression and of its necessary relation to resistance, by a rough analogy derived from our actual situation at the present moment. Let us suppose that in this lecture-room and among this audience, whose exemplary quiet and attentiveness I cannot sufficiently commend, there is nevertheless someone who is causing a disturbance and whose ill-mannered laughter, chattering and shuffling with his feet are distracting my attention from my task. I have to announce that I cannot proceed with my lecture; and thereupon three or four of you who are strong men stand up and, after a short struggle, put the interrupter outside the door. So now he is 'repressed', and I can continue my lecture. But in order that the interruption shall not be repeated, in case the individual who has been expelled should try to enter the room once more, the gentlemen who have put my will into effect place their chairs up against the door and thus establish a 'resistance' after the repression has been accomplished. If you will now translate the two localities concerned into psychical terms as the 'conscious' and the 'unconscious', you will have before you a fairly good picture of the process of repression.

You will now see in what it is that the difference lies between our view and Janet's. We do not derive the psychical splitting from an innate incapacity for synthesis on the part of the mental apparatus; we explain it dynamically, from the conflict of opposing mental forces and recognize it as the outcome of an active struggling on the part of the two psychical groupings against each other. But our view gives rise to a large number of fresh problems. Situations of mental conflict are, of course, exceedingly common; efforts by the ego to ward off painful memories are quite regularly to be observed without their producing the result of a mental split. The reflection cannot be escaped that further determinants must be present if the conflict is to lead to dissociation. I will also readily grant you that the hypothesis of repression leaves us not at the end but at the beginning of a psychological theory. We can only go forward step by step however, and complete knowledge must await the results of further and deeper researches.

Nor is it advisable to attempt to explain the case of Breuer's patient from the point of view of repression. That case history is not suited to this purpose, because its findings were reached with the help of hypnotic influence. It is only if you exclude hypnosis that you can observe resistances and repressions and form an adequate idea of the truly pathogenic course of events. Hypnosis conceals the resistance and renders a certain area of the mind accessible; but, as against this, it builds up the resistance at the frontiers of this area into a wall that makes everything beyond it inaccessible.

Our most valuable lesson from Breuer's observation was what it proved concerning the relation between symptoms and pathogenic experiences or psychical traumas, and we must not omit now to consider these discoveries from the standpoint of the theory of repression. At first sight it really seems impossible to trace a path from repression to the formation of symptoms. Instead of giving a complicated theoretical account, I will return here to the analogy which I employed earlier for my explanation of repression. If you come to think of it, the removal of the interrupter and the posting of the guardians at the door may not mean the end of the story. It may very well be that the individual who has been expelled, and who has now become embittered and reckless, will cause us further trouble. It is true that he is no longer among us; we are free from his presence, from his insulting laughter and his *sotto voce* comments. But in some respects, nevertheless, the repression has been unsuccessful; for now he is making an intolerable exhibition of himself outside the room, and his shouting and banging on the door with his fists interfere with my lecture even more than his bad behaviour did before. In these circumstances we could not fail to be delighted if our respected president, Dr. Stanley Hall, should be willing to assume the role of mediator and peacemaker. He would have a talk with the unruly person outside and would then come to us with a request that he should be re-admitted after all: he himself would guarantee that the man would now behave better. On Dr. Hall's authority we decide to lift the repression, and peace and quiet are restored. This presents what is really no bad picture of the physician's task in the psycho-analytic treatment of the neuroses.

To put the matter more directly. The investigation of hysterical patients and of other neurotics leads us to the conclusion that their repression of the idea to which the intolerable wish is attached has been a *failure.* It is true that they have driven it out of consciousness and out of memory and have apparently saved themselves a large amount of unpleasure. *But the repressed wishful impulse continues to exist in the unconscious.* It is on the look-out for an opportunity of being activated, and when that happens it succeeds in sending into consciousness a disguised and unrecognizable *substitute* for what had been repressed, and to this there soon become attached the same feelings of unpleasure which it was hoped had been saved by the repression. This substitute for the repressed idea—the *symptom*—is proof against further attacks from the defensive ego; and in place of the short conflict an ailment now appears which is not brought to an end by the passage of time. Alongside the indication of distortion in the symptom, we can trace in it the remains of some kind of indirect resemblance to the idea that was originally repressed. The paths along which the substitution was effected can be traced in the course of the patient's psycho-analytic treatment; and in order to bring about recovery, the symptom must be led back along the same paths and once more turned into the repressed idea. If what was repressed is brought back again into conscious mental activity—a process which presupposes the overcoming of considerable resistances—the resulting psychical conflict, which the patient had tried to avoid, can, under the physician's guidance, reach a better outcome than was offered by repression. There are a number of such opportune solutions, which may bring the conflict and the neurosis to a happy end, and which may in certain instances be combined. The patient's personality may be convinced that it has been wrong in rejecting the pathogenic wish and may be led into accepting it wholly or in part; or the wish itself may be directed to a higher and consequently unobjectionable aim (this is what we call its 'sublimation'); or the rejection of the wish may be recognized as a justifiable one, but the automatic and therefore inefficient mechanism of repression may be replaced by a condemning judgement with the help of the highest human mental functions—conscious control of the wish is attained.

You must forgive me if I have not succeeded in giving you a more clearly intelligible account of these basic positions adopted by the method of treatment that is now described as 'psycho-analysis'. The difficulties have not lain only in the novelty of the subject. The nature of the incompatible wishes which, in spite of repression, succeed in making their existence in the unconscious perceptible, and the subjective and constitutional determinants which must be present in anyone before a failure of repression can occur and a substitute or symptom be formed—on all this I shall have more light to throw in some of my later observations.

Third Lecture

Ladies and Gentlemen,—It is not always easy to tell the truth, especially when one has to be concise; and I am thus to-day obliged to correct a wrong statement that I made in my last lecture. I said to you that, having dispensed with hypnosis, I insisted on my patients nevertheless telling me what occurred to them in connection with the subject under discussion, and assured them that they really knew everything that they had ostensibly forgotten and that the idea that occurred to them[1] would infallibly contain what we were in search of; and I went on to say to you that I found that the first idea occurring to my patients did in fact produce the right thing and turned out to be the forgotten continuation of the memory. This, however, is not in general the case, and I only put the matter so simply for the sake of brevity. Actually it was only for the first few times that the right thing which had been forgotten turned up as a result of simple insistence on my part. When the procedure was carried further, ideas kept on emerging that could not

---

[1][The German word here is *'Einfall'*, which is often translated 'association'; but the latter is a question-begging word and is avoided here as far as possible, even at the price of such long paraphrases as the present one. When, however, we come to *'freier Einfall'*, 'free association' (though still objectionable) is hardly to be escaped.]

be the right ones, since they were not appropriate and were rejected as being wrong by the patients themselves. Insistence was of no further help at this point, and I found myself once more regretting my abandonment of hypnosis.

While I was thus at a loss, I clung to a prejudice the scientific justification for which was proved years later by my friend C. G. Jung and his pupils in Zurich. I am bound to say that it is sometimes most useful to have prejudices. I cherished a high opinion of the strictness with which mental processes are determined, and I found it impossible to believe that an idea produced by a patient while his attention was on the stretch could be an arbitrary one and unrelated to the idea we were in search of. The fact that the two ideas were not identical could be satisfactorily explained from the postulated psychological state of affairs. In the patient under treatment two forces were in operation against each other: on the one hand, his conscious endeavour to bring into consciousness the forgotten idea in his unconscious, and on the other hand, the resistance we already know about, which was striving to prevent what was repressed or its derivatives from thus becoming conscious. If this resistance amounted to little or nothing, what had been forgotten became conscious without distortion. It was accordingly plausible to suppose that the greater the resistance against what we were in search of becoming conscious, the greater would be its distortion. The idea which occurred to the patient in place of what we were in search of had thus itself originated like a symptom: it was a new, artificial and ephemeral substitute for what had been repressed, and was dissimilar to it in proportion to the degree of distortion it had undergone under the influence of the resistance. But, owing to its nature as a symptom, it must nevertheless have a certain similarity to what we were in search of; and if the resistance were not too great, we ought to be able to guess the latter from the former. The idea occurring to the patient must be in the nature of an *allusion* to the repressed element, like a representation of it in indirect speech.

We know cases in the field of normal mental life in which situations analogous to the one we have just assumed produce similar results. One such case is that of jokes. The problems of psycho-analytic technique have compelled me to investigate the technique of making jokes. I will give you one example of this—incidentally, a joke in English.

This is the anecdote.[2] Two not particularly scrupulous business men had succeeded, by dint of a series of highly risky enterprises, in amassing a large fortune, and they were now making efforts to push their way into good society. One method, which struck them as a likely one, was to have their portraits painted by the most celebrated and highly-paid artist in the city, whose pictures had an immense reputation. The precious canvases were shown for the first time at a large evening party, and the two hosts themselves led the most influential connoisseur and art critic up to the wall on which the portraits were hanging side by side. He studied the works for a long time, and then, shaking his head, as though there was something he had missed, pointed to the gap between the pictures and asked quietly: 'But where's the Saviour?'[3] I see you are all much amused at this joke. Let us now proceed to examine it. Clearly what the connoisseur meant to say was: 'You are a couple of rogues, like the two thieves between whom the Saviour was crucified.' But he did not say this. Instead he made a remark which seems at first sight strangely inappropriate and irrelevant, but which we

---

[2]Cf. *Jokes and their Relation to the Unconscious*, 1905c [Chapter II, Section 11, where the story is discussed at greater length and, incidentally, described as an American one].
[3][In English in the original.]

recognize a moment later as an *allusion* to the insult that he had in mind and as a perfect substitute for it. We cannot expect to find in jokes *all* the characteristics that we have attributed to the ideas occurring to our patients, but we must stress the identity of the *motive* for the joke and for the idea. Why did the critic not tell the rogues straight out what he wanted to say? Because he had excellent counter-motives working against his desire to say it to their faces. There are risks attendant upon insulting people who are one's hosts and who have at their command the fists of a large domestic staff. One might easily meet with the fate which I suggested in my last lecture as an analogy for repression. That was the reason why the critic did not express the insult he had in mind directly but in the form of an 'allusion accompanied by omission'[4]; and the same state of things is responsible for our patients' producing a more or less distorted *substitute* instead of the forgotten idea we are in search of.

It is highly convenient, Ladies and Gentlemen, to follow the Zurich school (Bleuler, Jung, etc.) in describing a group of interdependent ideational elements cathected with affect as a 'complex'. We see, then, that if in our search for a repressed complex in one of our patients we start out from the last thing he remembers, we shall have every prospect of discovering the complex, provided that the patient puts a sufficient number of his free associations[5] at our disposal. Accordingly, we allow the patient to say whatever he likes, and hold fast to the postulate that nothing can occur to him which is not in an indirect fashion dependent on the com-

---

[4][This is one of the particular techniques described in the passage in Freud's book on jokes where the present anecdote occurs.]
[5][See footnote p. 29.]

plex we are in search of. If this method of discovering what is repressed strikes you as unduly circumstantial, I can at least assure you that it is the only practicable one.

When we come to putting this procedure into effect, we are subject to yet another interference. For the patient will often pause and come to a stop, and assert that he can think of nothing to say, and that nothing whatever occurs to his mind. If this were so and if the patient were right, then our procedure would once again have proved ineffective. But closer observation shows that such a stoppage of the flow of ideas never in fact occurs. It *appears* to happen only because the patient holds back or gets rid of the idea that he has become aware of, under the influence of the resistances which disguise themselves as various critical judgements about the value of the idea that has occurred to him. We can protect ourselves against this by warning him beforehand of this behaviour and requiring him to take no notice of such criticisms. He must, we tell him, entirely renounce any critical selection of this kind and say whatever comes into his head, even if he considers it incorrect or irrelevant or nonsensical, and above all if he finds it disagreeable to let himself think about what has occurred to him. So long as this ordinance is carried out we are certain of obtaining the material which will put us on the track of the repressed complexes.

This associative material, which the patient contemptuously rejects when he is under the influence of the resistance instead of under the doctor's, serves the psycho-analyst, as it were, as ore from which, with the help of some simple interpretative devices, he extracts its content of precious metal. If you are anxious to gain a rapid and provisional knowledge of a patient's repressed complexes, without as yet entering into their arrangement and interconnection, you will employ as a method of examination the 'association experiment' as it has been developed by Jung (1906) and his pupils. This procedure offers the psycho-analyst what qualitative analysis offers the chemist. In the treatment of neurotic patients it can be dispensed with; but it is indispensable for the objective demonstration of complexes and in the examination of the psychoses, which has been embarked on with so much success by the Zurich school.

Working over the ideas that occur to patients when they submit to the main rule of psycho-analysis is not our only technical method of discovering the unconscious. The same purpose is served by two other procedures: the interpretation of patients' dreams and the exploitation of their faulty and haphazard actions.

I must admit, Ladies and Gentlemen, that I hesitated for a long time whether, instead of giving you this condensed general survey of the whole field of psycho-analysis, it might not be better to present you with a detailed account of dream-interpretation.[6] I was held back by a purely subjective and seemingly secondary motive. It seemed to me almost indecent in a country which is devoted to practical aims to make my appearance as a 'dream-interpreter', before you could possibly know the importance that can attach to that antiquated and derided art. The interpretation of dreams is in fact the royal road to a knowledge of the unconscious;[7] it is the securest foundation of psycho-analysis and the field in which every worker must acquire his convictions and seek his training. If I am asked how one can become a psychoanalyst, I reply: 'By studying one's own dreams.' Every opponent of psycho-analysis hitherto has, with a nice discrimina-

---

[6] *The Interpretation of Dreams* (1900a).
[7] [This phrase was introduced in almost identical words into the second (1909) edition of *The Interpretation of Dreams* (*Standard Ed.*, **5**, 608).]

tion, either evaded any consideration of *The Interpretation of Dreams*, or has sought to skirt over it with the most superficial objections. If, on the contrary, you can accept the solutions of the problems of dream-life, the novelties with which psycho-analysis confronts your minds will offer you no further difficulties.

You should bear in mind that the dreams which we produce at night have, on the one hand, the greatest external similarity and internal kinship with the creations of insanity, and are, on the other hand, compatible with complete health in waking life. There is nothing paradoxical in the assertion that no one who regards these 'normal' illusions, delusions and character-changes with astonishment instead of comprehension has the slightest prospect of understanding the abnormal structures of pathological mental states otherwise than as a layman. You may comfortably count almost all psychiatrists among such laymen.

I invite you now to follow me on a brief excursion through the region of dream-problems. When we are awake we are in the habit of treating dreams with the same contempt with which patients regard the associations that are demanded of them by the psycho-analyst. We dismiss them, too, by forgetting them as a rule, quickly and completely. Our low opinion of them is based on the strange character even of those dreams that are not confused and meaningless, and on the obvious absurdity and nonsensicalness of other dreams. Our dismissal of them is related to the uninhibited shamelessness and immorality of the tendencies openly exhibited in some dreams. It is well known that the ancient world did not share this low opinion of dreams. Nor are the lower strata of our own society to-day in any doubt about the value of dreams; like the peoples of antiquity, they expect them to reveal the future. I confess that I feel no necessity for making any mystical assumptions in order to fill the gaps in our present knowledge, and accordingly I have never been able to find anything to confirm the prophetic nature of dreams. There are plenty of other things—sufficiently wonderful too—to be said about them.

In the first place, not all dreams are alien to the dreamer, incomprehensible and confused. If you inspect the dreams of very young children, from eighteen months upwards, you will find them perfectly simple and easy to explain. Small children always dream of the fulfilment of wishes that were aroused in them the day before but not satisfied. You will need no interpretative art in order to find this simple solution; all you need do is to enquire into the child's experiences on the previous day (the 'dream-day'). Certainly the most satisfactory solution of the riddle of dreams would be to find that adults' dreams too were like those of children—fulfilments of wishful impulses that had come to them on the dream-day. And such in fact is the case. The difficulties in the way of this solution can be overcome step by step if dreams are analysed more closely.

The first and most serious objection is that the content of adults' dreams is as a rule unintelligible and could not look more unlike the fulfilment of a wish. And here is the answer. Such dreams have been subjected to distortion; the psychical process underlying them might originally have been expressed in words quite differently. You must distinguish the *manifest content of the dream,* as you vaguely recollect it in the morning and laboriously (and, as it seems, arbitrarily) clothe it in words, and the *latent dream-thoughts,* which you must suppose were present in the unconscious. This distortion in dreams is the same process that you have already come to know in investigating the formation of hysterical symptoms. It indicates, too, that the same interplay of mental forces is at work in the formation of dreams as in that of symptoms. The manifest content of the dream is the distorted substitute for the unconscious dream-thoughts and this distortion is the work of the ego's forces of defence—of resistances. In waking life these resistances altogether prevent the repressed wishes of the unconscious from entering consciousness; and during the lowered state of sleep they are at least strong enough to oblige them to adopt a veil of disguise. Thereafter, the dreamer can no more understand the meaning of his dreams than the hysteric can understand the connection and significance of his symptoms.

You can convince yourself that there are such things as latent dream-thoughts and that the relation between them and the manifest content of the dream is really as I have described it, if you carry out an analysis of dreams, the technique of which is the same as that of psycho-analysis. You entirely disregard the apparent connections between the elements in the manifest dream and collect the ideas that occur to you in connection with each separate element of the dream by free association according to the psycho-analytic rule of procedure. From this material you arrive at the latent dream-thoughts, just as you arrived at the patient's hidden complexes from his associations to his symptoms and memories. The latent dream-thoughts which have been reached in this way will at once show you how completely justified we have been in tracing back adults' dreams to children's dreams. The true meaning of the dream, which has now taken the place of its manifest content, is always clearly intelligible; it has its starting-point in experiences of the previous day, and proves to be a fulfilment of unsatisfied wishes. The manifest dream, which you know from your memory when you wake up, can therefore only be described as a *disguised* fulfilment of *repressed* wishes.

You can also obtain a view, by a kind of synthetic work, of the process which has brought about the distortion of the unconscious dream-thoughts into the manifest content of the dream. We call this process the 'dream-work'. It deserves our closest theoretical interest, since we are able to study in it, as nowhere else, what unsuspected psychical processes can occur in the unconscious, or rather, to put it more accurately, *between* two separate psychical systems like the conscious and unconscious. Among these freshly discovered psychical processes those of *condensation* and *displacement* are especially noticeable. The dream-work is a special case of the effects produced by two different mental groupings on each other—that is, of the consequences of mental splitting; and it seems identical in all essentials with the process of distortion which transforms the repressed complexes into symptoms where there is unsuccessful repression.

You will also learn with astonishment from the analysis of dreams (and most convincingly from that of your own) what an unsuspectedly great part is played in human development by impressions and experiences of early childhood. In dream-life the child that is in man pursues its existence, as it were, and retains all its characteristics and wishful impulses, even such as have become unserviceable in later life. There will be brought home to you with irresistible force the many developments, repressions, sublimations and reaction-formations, by means of which a child with a quite other innate endowment grows into what we call a normal man, the bearer, and in part the victim, of the civilization that has been so painfully acquired.

I should like you to notice, too, that the analysis of dreams has shown us that the unconscious makes use of a particular symbolism, especially for representing sexual complexes. This symbolism varies partly from individual to individual; but partly it is laid down in a typical form and seems to coincide with the symbolism which, as we suspect, underlies our myths and fairy tales. It seems not impossible that these creations of the popular mind might find an explanation through the help of dreams.

Lastly, I must warn you not to let yourselves be put out by the objection that the occurrence of anxiety-dreams contradicts our view of dreams as the fulfilments of wishes. Apart from the fact that these anxiety-dreams, like the rest, require interpretation before any judgement can be formed on them, it must be stated quite generally that the anxiety does not depend on the content of the dream in such a simple manner as one might imagine without having more knowledge and taking more account of the determinants of neurotic anxiety. Anxiety is one of the ego's reactions in repudiation of repressed wishes that have become powerful; and its occurrence in dreams as well is very easily explicable when the formation of the dream has been carried out with too much of an eye to the fulfilment of these repressed wishes.

As you see, research into dreams would be justified for its own sake merely by the information it gives us on matters that can with difficulty be discovered in other ways. But we were in fact led to the subject in connection with the psycho-analytic treatment of neurotics. You will easily understand from what I have already said how it is that dream-interpretation, if it is not made too difficult by the patient's resistances, leads to a knowledge of his hidden and repressed wishes and of the complexes nourished by them; and I can now pass on to the third group of mental phenomena whose study has become one of the technical instruments of psycho-analysis.

The phenomena in question are the small faulty actions performed by both normal and neurotic people, to which as a rule no importance is attached: forgetting things that might be known and sometimes in fact *are* known (e.g. the occasional difficulty in recalling proper names), slips of the tongue in talking, by which we ourselves are so often affected, analogous slips of the pen and misreadings, bungling the performance of actions, losing objects or breaking them. All of these are things for which as a rule no psychological determinants are sought and which are allowed to pass without criticism as consequences of distraction or inattention or similar causes. Besides these there are the actions and gestures which people carry out without noticing them at all, to say nothing of attributing any psychological importance to them: playing about and fiddling with things, humming tunes, fingering parts of one's own body or one's clothing and so on.[8] These small things, faulty actions and symptomatic or haphazard actions alike, are not so insignificant as people, by a sort of conspiracy of silence, are ready to suppose. They always have a meaning, which can usually be interpreted with ease and certainty from the situation in which they occur. And it turns out that once again they give expression to impulses and intentions which have to be kept back and hidden from one's own consciousness, or that they are actually derived from the same repressed wishful impulses and complexes which we have already come to know as the creators of symptoms and the constructors of dreams. They therefore deserve to be rated as symptoms, and if they are examined they may lead, just as dreams do, to the uncovering of the hidden part of the mind. A man's most intimate secrets are as a rule betrayed by their help. If they occur particularly easily and frequently even in healthy people in whom the repression of unconscious impulses has on the whole been quite successful, they have their triviality and inconspicuousness to thank for it. But they can claim a high theoretical

---

[8]Cf. *The Psychopathology of Everyday Life* (1901*b*).

value, since they prove that repression and the formation of substitutes occur even under healthy conditions.

As you already see, psycho-analysts are marked by a particularly strict belief in the determination of mental life. For them there is nothing trivial, nothing arbitrary or haphazard. They expect in every case to find sufficient motives where, as a rule, no such expectation is raised. Indeed, they are prepared to find *several* motives for one and the same mental occurrence, whereas what seems to be our innate craving for causality declares itself satisfied with a *single* psychical cause.

If you will now bring together the means we possess for uncovering what is concealed, forgotten and repressed in the mind (the study of the ideas occurring to patients under free association, of their dreams and of their faulty and symptomatic actions), and if you will add to these the exploitation of certain other phenomena which occur during psychoanalytic treatment and on which I shall have a few remarks to make later under the heading of 'transference'—if you bear all these in mind, you will agree with me in concluding that our technique is already efficient enough to fulfil its task, to bring the pathogenic psychical material into consciousness and so to get rid of the ailments that have been brought about by the formation of substitutive symptoms. And if, in the course of our therapeutic endeavours, we extend and deepen our knowledge of the human mind both in health and sickness, that can, of course, only be regarded as a peculiar attraction in our work.

You may have formed an impression that the technique through whose armoury I have just conducted you is particularly difficult. In my opinion that technique is entirely in conformity with the material with which it has to deal. But this much at least is clear: it is not a self-evident one and it must be learnt just as the techniques of histology or surgery must be learnt. You will perhaps be surprised to hear that in Europe we have heard a large number of judgements on psycho-analysis from people who know nothing of this technique and do not employ it; and who go on to demand with apparent scorn that we shall prove to them the correctness of our findings. Among these adversaries there are no doubt some to whom a scientific mode of thought is not as a rule alien, who, for instance, would not reject the results of a microscopic examination because it could not be confirmed on the anatomical preparation with the naked eye, but who would first form a judgement on the matter themselves with the help of a microscope. But, where psycho-analysis is concerned, the prospects of recognition are in truth less favourable. Psycho-analysis is seeking to bring to conscious recognition the things in mental life which are repressed; and everyone who forms a judgement on it is himself a human being, who possesses similar repressions and may perhaps be maintaining them with difficulty. They are therefore bound to call up the same resistance in him as in our patients; and that resistance finds it easy to disguise itself as an intellectual rejection and to bring up arguments like those which we ward off in our patients by means of the fundamental rule of psycho-analysis. We often become aware in our opponents, just as we do in our patients, that their power of judgement is very noticeably influenced affectively in the sense of being diminished. The arrogance of consciousness (in rejecting dreams with such contempt, for instance) is one of the most powerful of the devices with which we are provided as a universal protection against the incursion of unconscious complexes. That is why it is so hard to convince people of the reality of the unconscious and to teach them to recognize something new which is in contradiction to their conscious knowledge.

Fourth Lecture

Ladies and Gentlemen,—You will want to know now what we have found out about the pathogenic complexes and repressed wishful impulses of neurotics with the help of the technical methods I have described.

First and foremost we have found out one thing. Psychoanalytic research traces back the symptoms of patients' illnesses with really surprising regularity to impressions from their *erotic life*. It shows us that the pathogenic wishful impulses are in the nature of erotic instinctual components; and it forces us to suppose that among the influences leading to the illness the predominant significance must be assigned to erotic disturbances, and that this is the case in both sexes.

I am aware that this assertion of mine will not be willingly believed. Even workers who are ready to follow my psychological studies are inclined to think that I over-estimate the part played by sexual factors; they meet me with the question why *other* mental excitations should not lead to the phenomena I have described of repression and the formation of substitutes. I can only answer that I do not know why they should not, and that I should have no objection to their doing so; but experience shows that they do not carry this weight, that at most they *support* the operation of the sexual factors but cannot replace them. Far from this position having been postulated by me theoretically, at the time of the joint publication of the *Studies* with Dr. Breuer in 1895 I had not yet adopted it; and I was only converted to it when my experiences became more numerous and penetrated into the subject more deeply. There are among my present audience a few of my closest friends and followers, who have travelled with me here to Worcester. Enquire from them, and you will hear that they all began by completely disbelieving my assertion that sexual aetiology was of decisive importance, until their own analytic experiences compelled them to accept it.

A conviction of the correctness of this thesis was not precisely made easier by the behaviour of patients. Instead of willingly presenting us with information about their sexual life, they try to conceal it by every means in their power. People are in general not candid over sexual matters. They do not show their sexuality freely, but to conceal it they wear a heavy overcoat woven of a tissue of lies, as though the weather were bad in the world of sexuality. Nor are they mistaken. It is a fact that sun and wind are not favourable to sexual activity in this civilized world of ours; none of us can reveal his erotism freely to others. But when your patients discover that they can feel quite easy about it while they are under your treatment, they discard this veil of lies, and only then are you in a position to form a judgement on this debatable question. Unluckily even doctors are not preferred above other human creatures in their personal relation to questions of sexual life, and many of them are under the spell of the combination of prudery and prurience which governs the attitude of most 'civilized people' in matters of sexuality.

Let me now proceed with my account of our findings. In another set of cases psycho-analytic investigation traces the symptoms back, it is true, not to sexual experiences but to commonplace traumatic ones. But this distinction loses its significance owing to another circumstance. For the work of analysis required for the thorough explanation and complete recovery of a case never comes to a stop at events that occurred at the time of the onset of the illness, but invariably goes back to the patient's puberty and early childhood; and it is only there that it comes upon the impressions and events which determined the later onset of the illness. It is only experiences in childhood that explain susceptibility to later traumas and it is only by uncovering these almost invariably forgotten memory-traces and by making them conscious that we acquire the power to get rid of the symptoms. And here we reach the same conclusion as in our investigation of dreams: the imperishable, repressed wishful impulses of childhood have alone provided the power for the construction of symptoms, and without them the reaction to later traumas would have taken a normal course. But these powerful wishful impulses of childhood may without exception be described as sexual.

And now at last I am quite certain that I have surprised you. 'Is there such a thing, then, as infantile sexuality?' you will ask 'Is not childhood on the contrary the period of life that is marked by the absence of the sexual instinct?' No, Gentlemen, it is certainly not the case that the sexual instinct enters into children at the age of puberty in the way in which, in the Gospel, the devil entered into the swine. A child has its sexual instincts and activities from the first; it comes into the world with them; and, after an important course of development passing through many stages, they lead to what is known as the normal sexuality of the adult. There is even no difficulty in observing the manifestations of these sexual activities in children; on the contrary, it calls for some skill to overlook them or explain them away.

By a lucky chance I am in a position to call a witness in favour of my assertions from your very midst. I have here in my hand a paper written by a Dr. Sanford Bell, which was published in *The American Journal of Psychology* in 1902. The author is a Fellow of Clark University, of the very institution in whose lecture-room we are now assembled. In this work, which is entitled 'A Preliminary Study of the Emotion of Love between the Sexes', and which appeared three years before my *Three Essays on the Theory of Sexuality* [1905d], the author says exactly what I have just told you: 'The emotion of sex-love . . . does not make its appearance for the first time at the period of adolescence, as has been thought.' He carried out his work in what we in Europe would call 'the American manner', collecting no fewer than 2,500 positive observations in the course of fifteen years, among them 800 of his own. Concerning the signs by which these instances of falling in love are revealed he writes as follows: 'The unprejudiced mind in observing these manifestations in hundreds of couples of children cannot escape referring them to sex origin. The most exacting mind is satisfied when to these observations are added the confessions of those who have, as children, experienced the emotion to a marked degree of intensity and whose memories of childhood are relatively distinct.' But those of you who do not wish to believe in infantile sexuality will be most of all surprised to hear that not a few of these children who have fallen in love so early are of the tender age of three, four and five.

It would not astonish me if you were to attach more credence to these observations made by one of your closest neighbours than to mine. I myself have recently been fortunate enough to obtain a fairly complete picture of the somatic instinctual manifestations and mental products at an early stage of a child's erotic life from the analysis of a five-year-old boy, suffering from anxiety—an analysis carried out with a correct technique by his own father.[1] And I may remind you that only a few hours ago, in this same room, my friend Dr. C. G. Jung reported an observation to you made on a still younger girl who, with a precipitating cause similar to my patient's (the birth of a younger child in the family), made it possible to infer with certainty the presence of almost the same sensual impulses, wishes and complexes. [Cf. Jung, 1910.] I do not despair, therefore, of your becoming reconciled to what seems at first sight the strange idea of infantile sexuality. And I should like to quote to you the praiseworthy example of the Zurich psychiatrist, Dr. E. Bleuler, who declared publicly not many years ago that he was 'unable to comprehend my theories of sexuality', and who has since then confirmed the existence of infantile sexuality to its full extent from his own observations. (Cf. Bleuler, 1908.)

It is only too easy to explain why most people (whether medical observers or others) will hear nothing of the sexual life of children. They have forgotten their own infantile sexual activity under the pressure of their education to a civilized life, and they do not wish to be reminded of what has been repressed. They would arrive at other convictions if they were to begin their enquiry with a self-analysis, a revision and interpretation of their childhood memories.

Put away your doubts, then, and join me in a consideration of infantile sexuality from the earliest age.[2] A child's sexual instinct turns out to be put together out of a number of factors; it is capable of being divided up into numerous components which originate from various sources. Above

---

[1] 'The Analysis of a Phobia in a Five-Year-Old Boy' [Freud, 1909*b*].
[2] Cf. *Three Essays on the Theory of Sexuality* (1905*d*).

all, it is still independent of the reproductive function, into the service of which it will later be brought. It serves for the acquisition of different kinds of pleasurable feeling, which, basing ourselves on analogies and connections, we bring together under the idea of sexual pleasure. The chief source of infantile sexual pleasure is the appropriate excitation of certain parts of the body that are especially susceptible to stimulus: apart from the genitals, these are the oral, anal and urethral orifices, as well as the skin and other sensory surfaces. Since at this first phase of infantile sexual life satisfaction is obtained from the subject's own body and extraneous objects are disregarded, we term this phase (from a word coined by Havelock Ellis) that of *auto-erotism*. We call the parts of the body that are important in the acquisition of sexual pleasure 'erotogenic zones'. Thumb-sucking (or sensual sucking) in the youngest infants is a good example of this auto-erotic satisfaction from an erotogenic zone. The first scientific observer of this phenomenon, a paediatrician in Budapest named Lindner (1879), already interpreted it correctly as sexual satisfaction and described exhaustively its transition to other and higher forms of sexual activity. Another sexual satisfaction at this period of life is the masturbatory excitation of the genitals, which retains so much importance in later life and by many people is never completely conquered. Alongside these and other auto-erotic activities, we find in children at a very early age manifestations of those instinctual components of sexual pleasure (or, as we like to say, of libido) which presuppose the taking of an extraneous person as an object. These instincts occur in pairs of opposites, active and passive. I may mention as the most important representatives of this group the desire to cause pain (sadism) with its passive counterpart (masochism) and the active and passive desire for looking, from the former of which curiosity branches off later on and from the latter the impulsion to artistic and theatrical display. Others of a child's sexual activities already imply the making of an 'object-choice', where an extraneous person becomes the main feature, a person who owes his importance in the first instance to considerations arising from the self-preservative instinct. But at this early period of childhood difference in sex plays no decisive part as yet. Thus you can attribute some degree of homosexuality to every child without doing him an injustice. This widespread and copious but dissociated sexual life of children, in which each separate instinct pursues its own acquisition of pleasure independently of all the rest, is now brought together and organized in two main directions, so that by the end of puberty the individual's final sexual character is as a rule completely formed. On the one hand, the separate instincts become subordinated to the dominance of the genital zone, so that the whole sexual life enters the service of reproduction, and the satisfaction of the separate instincts retains its importance only as preparing for and encouraging the sexual act proper. On the other hand, object-choice pushes auto-erotism into the background, so that in the subject's erotic life all the components of the sexual instinct now seek satisfaction in relation to the person who is loved. Not all of the original sexual components, however, are admitted to take part in this final establishment of sexuality. Even before puberty extremely energetic repressions of certain instincts have been effected under the influence of education, and mental forces such as shame, disgust and morality have been set up, which, like watchmen, maintain these repressions. So that when at puberty the high tide of sexual demands is reached, it is met by these mental reactive or resistant structures like dams, which direct its flow into what are called normal channels and make it impossible for it to reactivate the instincts that have undergone repression. It is in particular the coprophilic impulses of childhood—that is to say, the desires attaching to the excreta—which are submitted the most rigorously to repression, and the same is true, furthermore, of fixation to the figures to which the child's original object-choice was attached.

There is a dictum in general pathology, Gentlemen, which asserts that every developmental process carries with it the seed of a pathological disposition, in so far as that process may be inhibited, delayed, or may run its course incompletely. The same thing is true of the highly complicated development of the sexual function. It does not occur smoothly in every individual; and, if not, it leaves behind it either abnormalities or a predisposition to fall ill later, along the path of involution (i.e. regression). It may happen that not all the component instincts submit to the dominance of the genital zone. An instinct which remains in this way independent leads to what we describe as a *perversion*, and may substitute its own sexual aim for the normal one. It very often happens, as I have already said, that auto-erotism is not completely conquered, and evidence of this is given by a great variety of subsequent disturbances. The originally equal value attached to the two sexes as sexual objects may persist, and this will lead to a tendency in adult life to homosexual activity, which can in certain circumstances be intensified into exclusive homosexuality. These classes of disturbance represent direct inhibitions in the development of the sexual function; they comprise the perversions and, what is by no means rare, general infantilism in sexual life.

The predisposition to *neurosis* is traceable to impaired sexual development in a different way. Neuroses are related to perversions as negative to positive. The same instinctual components as in the perversions can be observed in the neuroses as vehicles of complexes and constructors of symp-

toms, but in the latter case they operate from the unconscious. Thus they have undergone repression, but have been
able, in defiance of it, to persist in the unconscious. Psycho-
analysis makes it clear that an excessively strong manifestation of these instincts at a very early age leads to a kind of
partial *fixation*, which then constitutes a weak point in the
structure of the sexual function. If in maturity the performance of the normal sexual function comes up against obstacles, the repression that took place during the course of
development will be broken through at the precise points at
which the infantile fixations occurred.

But here you will perhaps protest that all this is not
sexuality. I have been using the word in a far wider sense
than that in which you have been accustomed to understand
it. So much I am quite ready to grant you. But the question
arises whether it is not rather you who have been using the
word in far too narrow a sense by restricting it to the sphere
of reproduction. It means that you are sacrificing an understanding of the perversions and the connection between the
perversions, the neuroses and normal sexual life; and you are
making it impossible for you to recognize in its true significance the easily observable beginnings of the somatic and
mental erotic life of children. But however you may choose
to decide the verbal usage, you should bear firmly in mind
that psycho-analysts understand sexuality in the full sense to
which one is led by a consideration of infantile sexuality.

Let us return to the sexual development of children. We
have some arrears to make up owing to our having paid more
atten tion to the somatic than to the mental phenomena of
sexual life. The child's first choice of an object, which de-
rives from its need for help, claims our further interest. Its
choice is directed in the first instance to all those who look
after it, but these soon give place to its parents. Children's

relations to their parents, as we learn alike from direct observations of children and from later analytic examination of adults, are by no means free from elements of accompanying sexual excitation. The child takes both of its parents, and more particularly one of them, as the object of its erotic wishes. In so doing, it usually follows some indication from its parents, whose affection bears the clearest characteristics of a sexual activity, even though of one that is inhibited in its aims. As a rule a father prefers his daughter and a mother her son; the child reacts to this by wishing, if he is a son, to take his father's place, and, if she is a daughter, her mother's. The feelings which are aroused in these relations between parents and children and in the resulting ones between brothers and sisters are not only of a positive or affectionate kind but also of a negative or hostile one. The complex which is thus formed is doomed to early repression; but it continues to exercise a great and lasting influence from the unconscious. It is to be suspected that, together with its extensions, it constitutes the *nuclear complex* of every neurosis, and we may expect to find it no less actively at work in other regions of mental life. The myth of King Oedipus, who killed his father and took his mother to wife, reveals, with little modification, the infantile wish, which is later opposed and repudiated by the *barrier against incest.* Shakespeare's *Hamlet* is equally rooted in the soil of the incest-complex, but under a better disguise.[3]

During the time when the child is dominated by the still unrepressed nuclear complex, an important part of his intellectual activity is brought into the service of his sexual interests. He begins to enquire where babies come from, and, on

[3][Freud adopted the term 'Oedipus complex' for the first time shortly after these lectures were delivered, in the first of his 'Contributions to the Psychology of Love' (1910*h*). See below, p. 171].

the basis of the evidence presented to him, guesses more of the true facts than the grown-ups imagine. His interest in these researches is usually set going by the very real threat offered to him by the arrival of a new baby, which to begin with he regards merely as a competitor. Under the influence of the component instincts that are active in himself, he arrives at a number of 'infantile sexual theories'—such as attributing a male genital organ to both sexes alike, or supposing that babies are conceived by eating and born through the end of the bowel, or regarding sexual intercourse as a hostile act, a kind of violent subjugation. But as a result precisely of the incompleteness of his sexual constitution, and of the gap in his knowledge due to the hidden nature of the female sexual channel, the young investigator is obliged to abandon his work as a failure. The fact of this childish research itself, as well as the different infantile sexual theories that it brings to light, remain of importance in determining the formation of the child's character and the content of any later neurotic illness.

It is inevitable and perfectly normal that a child should take his parents as the first objects of his love. But his libido should not remain fixated to these first objects; later on, it should merely take them as a model, and should make a gradual transition from them on to extraneous people when the time for the final choice of an object arrives. The detachment of the child from his parents is thus a task that cannot be evaded if the young individual's social fitness is not to be endangered. During the time at which repression is making its selection among the component instincts, and later, when there should be a slackening of the parents' influence, which is essentially responsible for the expenditure of energy on these repressions, the task of education meets with great problems, which at the present time are certainly not always dealt with in an understanding and unobjectionable manner.

You must not suppose, Ladies and Gentlemen, that these discussions on sexual life and the psychosexual development of children have led us too far from psycho-analysis and the problem of curing nervous disorders. You can, if you like, regard psycho-analytic treatment as no more than a prolongation of education for the purpose of overcoming the residues of childhood.

Fifth Lecture

Ladies and Gentlemen,—With the discovery of infantile sexuality and the tracing back of neurotic symptoms to erotic instinctual components we have arrived at some unexpected formulas concerning the nature and purposes of neurotic illnesses. We see that human beings fall ill when, as a result of external obstacles or of an internal lack of adaptation, the satisfaction of their erotic needs *in reality* is frustrated. We see that they then take flight into *illness* in order that by its help they may find a satisfaction to take the place of what has been frustrated. We recognize that the pathological symptoms constitute a portion of the subject's sexual activity or even the whole of his sexual life, and we find that the withdrawal from reality is the main purpose of the illness but also the main damage caused by it. We suspect that our patients' resistance to recovery is no simple one, but compounded of several motives. Not only does the patient's ego rebel against giving up the repressions by means of which it has risen above its original disposition, but the sexual instincts are unwilling to renounce their substitutive satisfaction so long as it is uncertain whether reality will offer them anything better.

The flight from unsatisfactory reality into what, on account of the biological damage involved, we call illness

(though it is never without an immediate yield of pleasure
to the patient) takes place along the path of involution, of
regression, of a return to earlier phases of sexual life, phases
from which at one time satisfaction was not withheld. This
regression appears to be a twofold one: a *temporal* one, in
so far as the libido, the erotic needs, hark back to stages of
development that are earlier in time, and a *formal* one, in
that the original and primitive methods of psychical expression are employed in manifesting those needs. Both these
kinds of regression, however, lead back to childhood and
unite in bringing about an infantile condition of sexual life.

The deeper you penetrate into the pathogenesis of nervous illness, the more you will find revealed the connection
between the neuroses and other productions of the human
mind, including the most valuable. You will be taught that
we humans, with the high standards of our civilization and
under the pressure of our internal repressions, find reality
unsatisfying quite generally, and for that reason entertain a
life of phantasy in which we like to make up for the insuf-
ficiencies of reality by the production of wish-fulfilments.
These phantasies include a great deal of the true constitutional essence of the subject's personality as well as of those
of his impulses which are repressed where reality is concerned. The energetic and successful man is one who succeeds by his efforts in turning his wishful phantasies into
reality. Where this fails, as a result of the resistances of the
external world and of the subject's own weakness, he begins
to turn away from reality and withdraws into his more satis-
fying world of phantasy, the content of which is transformed
into symptoms should he fall ill. In certain favourable circumstances, it still remains possible for him to find another
path leading from these phantasies to reality, instead of
becoming permanently estranged from it by regressing to
infancy. If a person who is at loggerheads with reality pos-

sesses an *artistic gift* (a thing that is still a psychological mystery to us), he can transform his phantasies into artistic creations instead of into symptoms. In this manner he can escape the doom of neurosis and by this roundabout path regain his contact with reality. (Cf. Rank, 1907.) If there is persistent rebellion against the real world and if this precious gift is absent or insufficient, it is almost inevitable that the libido, keeping to the sources of the phantasies, will follow the path of regression, and will revive infantile wishes and end in neurosis. To-day neurosis takes the place of the monasteries which used to be the refuge of all whom life had disappointed or who felt too weak to face it.

Let me at this point state the principal finding to which we have been led by the psycho-analytic investigation of neurotics. The neuroses have no psychical content that is peculiar to them and that might not equally be found in healthy people. Or, as Jung has expressed it, neurotics fall ill of the same complexes against which we healthy people struggle as well. Whether that struggle ends in health, in neurosis, or in a countervailing superiority of achievement, depends on *quantitative* considerations, on the relative strength of the conflicting forces.

I have not yet told you, Ladies and Gentlemen, of the most important of the observations which confirm our hypothesis of the sexual instinctual forces operating in neuroses. In every psycho-analytic treatment of a neurotic patient the strange phenomenon that is known as 'transference' makes its appearance. The patient, that is to say, directs towards the physician a degree of affectionate feeling (mingled, often enough, with hostility) which is based on no real relation between them and which—as is shown by every detail of its emergence—can only be traced back to old wishful phantasies of the patient's which have become unconscious. Thus the part of the patient's emotional life which he can no longer recall to memory is re-experienced by him in his relation to the physician; and it is only this re-experiencing in the 'transference' that convinces him of the existence and of the power of these unconscious sexual impulses. His symptoms, to take an analogy from chemistry, are precipitates of earlier experiences in the sphere of love (in the widest sense of the word), and it is only in the raised temperature of his experience of the transference that they can be resolved and reduced to other psychical products. In this reaction the physician, if I may borrow an apt phrase from Ferenczi (1909), plays the part of a catalytic ferment, which temporarily attracts to itself the affects liberated in the process. A study of transference, too, can give you the key to an understanding of hypnotic suggestion, which we employed to begin with as a technical method for investigating the unconscious in our patients. At that time hypnosis was found to be a help therapeutically, but a hindrance to the scientific understanding of the facts; for it cleared away the psychical resistances in a certain area while building them up into an unscalable wall at its frontiers. You must not suppose, moreover, that the phenomenon of transference (of which, unfortunately, I can tell you all too little to-day) is *created* by psycho-analytic influence. Transference arises spontaneously in all human relationships just as it does between the patient and the physician. It is everywhere the true vehicle of therapeutic influence; and the less its presence is suspected, the more powerfully it operates. So psycho-analysis does not create it, but merely reveals it to consciousness and gains control of it in order to guide psychical processes towards the desired goal. I cannot, however, leave the topic of transference without stressing the fact that this phenomenon plays a decisive part in bringing conviction not only to the patient but also to the physi-

cian. I know it to be true of all my followers that they were
only convinced of the correctness of my assertions on the
pathogenesis of the neuroses by their experiences with transference; and I can very well understand that such certainty
of judgement cannot be attained before one has carried out
psycho-analyses and has oneself observed the workings of
transference.

Ladies and Gentlemen, from the intellectual point of
view we must, I think, take into account two special obstacles to recognizing psycho-analytic trains of thought. In the
first place, people are unaccustomed to reckoning with a
strict and universal application of determinism to mental
life; and in the second place, they are ignorant of the
peculiarities which distinguish unconscious mental processes from the conscious ones that are familiar to us. One
of the most widespread resistances to psycho-analytic work,
in the sick and healthy alike, can be traced to the second of
these two factors. People are afraid of doing harm by psycho-
analysis; they are afraid of bringing the repressed sexual
instincts into the patient's consciousness, as though that
involved a danger of their overwhelming his higher ethical
trends and of their robbing him of his cultural acquisitions.[1]
People notice that the patient has sore spots in his mind, but
shrink from touching them for fear of increasing his suffer-
ings. We can accept this analogy. It is no doubt kinder not
to touch diseased spots if it can do nothing else but cause
pain. But, as we know, a surgeon does not refrain from
examining and handling a focus of disease, if he is intending
to take active measures which he believes will lead to a
permanent cure. No one thinks of blaming him for the

---

[1][The last nine words are omitted, probably by an oversight, in the *Gesammelte Schriften* (1924) and *Gesammelte Werke* (1942).]

inevitable suffering caused by the examination or for the reactions to the operation, if only it gains its end and the patient achieves a lasting recovery as a result of the temporary worsening of his state. The case is similar with psychoanalysis. It may make the same claims as surgery: the increase in suffering which it causes the patient during treatment is incomparably less than what a surgeon causes, and is quite negligible in proportion to the severity of the underlying ailment. On the other hand, the final outcome that is so much dreaded—the destruction of the patient's cultural character by the instincts which have been set free from repression—is totally impossible. For alarm on this score takes no account of what our experiences have taught us with certainty—namely that the mental and somatic power of a wishful impulse, when once its repression has failed, is far stronger if it is unconscious than if it is conscious; so that to make it conscious can only be to weaken it. An unconscious wish cannot be influenced and it is independent of any contrary tendencies, whereas a conscious one is inhibited by whatever else is conscious and opposed to it. Thus the work of psycho-analysis puts itself at the orders of precisely the highest and most valuable cultural trends, as a better substitute for the unsuccessful repression.

What, then, becomes of the unconscious wishes which have been set free by psycho-analysis? Along what paths do we succeed in making them harmless to the subject's life? There are several such paths. The most frequent outcome is that, while the work is actually going on, these wishes are destroyed by the rational mental activity of the better impulses that are opposed to them. *Repression* is replaced by a *condemning judgement* carried out along the best lines. That is possible because what we have to get rid of is to a great extent only the consequences arising from earlier stages of the ego's development. The subject only succeeded in the past in repressing the unserviceable instinct because he himself was at that time still imperfectly organized and feeble. In his present-day maturity and strength, he will perhaps be able to master what is hostile to him with complete success.

A second outcome of the work of psycho-analysis is that it then becomes possible for the unconscious instincts revealed by it to be employed for the useful purposes which they would have found earlier if development had not been interrupted. For the extirpation of the infantile wishful impulses is by no means the ideal aim of development. Owing to their repressions, neurotics have sacrificed many sources of mental energy whose contributions would have been of great value in the formation of their character and in their activity in life. We know of a far more expedient process of development, called 'sublimation', in which the energy of the infantile wishful impulses is not cut off but remains ready for use—the unserviceable aim of the various impulses being replaced by one that is higher, and perhaps no longer sexual. It happens to be precisely the components of the *sexual* instinct that are specially marked by a capacity of this kind for sublimation, for exchanging their sexual aim for another one which is comparatively remote and socially valuable. It is probable that we owe our highest cultural successes to the contributions of energy made in this way to our mental functions. Premature repression makes the sublimation of the repressed instinct impossible; when the repression is lifted, the path to sublimation becomes free once more.

We must not omit to consider the third of the possible outcomes of the work of psycho-analysis. A certain portion of the repressed libidinal impulses has a claim to direct satisfaction and ought to find it in life. Our civilized standards make life too difficult for the majority of human organizations. Those standards consequently encourage the retreat from reality and the generating of neuroses, without achieving any surplus of cultural gain by this excess of sexual repression. We ought not to exalt ourselves so high as completely to neglect what was originally animal in our nature. Nor should we forget that the satisfaction of the individual's happiness cannot be erased from among the aims of our civilization. The plasticity of the components of sexuality, shown by their capacity for sublimation, may indeed offer a great temptation to strive for still greater cultural achievements by still further sublimation. But, just as we do not count on our machines converting more than a certain fraction of the heat consumed into useful mechanical work, we ought not to seek to alienate the whole amount of the energy of the sexual instinct from its proper ends. We cannot succeed in doing so; and if the restriction upon sexuality were to be carried too far it would inevitably bring with it all the evils of soil-exhaustion.

It may be that you for your part will regard the warning with which I close as an exaggeration. I shall only venture on an indirect picture of my conviction by telling you an old story and leaving you to make what use you like of it. German literature is familiar with a little town called Schilda, to whose inhabitants clever tricks of every possible sort are attributed. The citizens of Schilda, so we are told, possessed a horse with whose feats of strength they were highly pleased and against which they had only one objection—that it consumed such a large quantity of expensive oats. They determined to break it of this bad habit very gently by reducing its ration by a few stalks every day, till they had accustomed it to complete abstinence. For a time things went excellently: the horse was weaned to the point of eating only one stalk a day, and on the succeeding day it was at length to work without any oats at all. On the morning of that day the spiteful animal was found dead; and the citizens of Schilda could not make out what it had died of.

We should be inclined to think that the horse was starved and that no work at all could be expected of an animal without a certain modicum of oats.

I must thank you for your invitation and for the attention with which you have listened to me.

APPENDIX

List of Expository Works by Freud

LIST OF ABBREVIATIONS

G.S. = Freud, *Gesammelte Schriften* (12 vols.), Vienna, 1924–34

G.W. = Freud, *Gesammelte Werke* (18 vols.), London, from 1940

C.P. = Freud, *Collected Papers* (5 vols.), London, 1924–50

Standard Ed. = Freud, *Standard Edition* (24 vols.), London, from 1953

S.K.S.N. = Freud, *Sammlung kleiner Schriften zur Neurosenlehre* (5 vols.), Vienna, 1906–22

S.P.H. = *Selected Papers on Hysteria and Other Psychoneuroses*, New York, 1909–20

Neurosenlehre und Technik = Freud, *Schriften zur Neurosenlehre und zur psychoanalytischen Technik (1913–1926)*, Vienna, 1931

Sexualtheorie und Traumlehre = Freud, *Kleine Schriften zur Sexualtheorie und zur Traumlehre*, Vienna, 1931

Technik und Metapsychol. = Freud, *Zur Technik der Psychoanalyse und zur Metapsychologie*, Vienna, 1924

BIBLIOGRAPHY
AND AUTHOR INDEX

[TITLES of books and periodicals are in italics; titles of papers are in inverted commas. Abbreviations are in accordance with the *World List of Scientific Periodicals* (London, 1952). Further abbreviations used in this volume will be found in the List at the end of the text. Numerals in thick type refer to volumes; ordinary numerals refer to pages. The figures in round brackets at the end of each entry indicate the page or pages of this volume on which the work in question is mentioned. In the case of the Freud entries, the letters attached to the dates of publication are in accordance with the corresponding entries in the complete bibliography of Freud's writings to be included in the last volume of the *Standard Edition*.

For non-technical authors, and for technical authors where no specific work is mentioned, see the General Index.]

BELL, J. SANFORD (1902) 'A Preliminary Study of the Emotion of Love between the Sexes', *Amer. J. Psychol.*, 13, 325 (45)

BLEULER, E. (1908) 'Sexuelle Abnormitäten der Kinder', *Jb. schweiz. Ges. SchulgesundPfl.*, 9, 623 (46)

BREUER, J., and FREUD, S. (1893) See FREUD, S. (1893a)
(1895) See FREUD, S. (1895d)

FERENCZI, S. (1909) 'Introjektion und Übertragung', *Jb. psychoan. psychopath. Forsch.*, 1, 422. (57)
[*Trans.:* 'Introjection and Transference', *First Contributions to Psycho-Analysis*, London, 1952, Chap. II.]

FREUD, S. (1893a) With BREUER, J., 'Über den psychischen Mechanismus hysterischer Phänomene: Vorläufige Mitteilung', *G.S.*, 1, 7; *G.W.*, 1, 81. (18)
[*Trans.:* 'On the Psychical Mechanism of Hysterical Phenomena: Preliminary Communication', *C.P.*, 1, 24; *Standard Ed.*, 2, 3.]

(1895*d*) With BREUER, J., *Studien über Hysterie*, Vienna. G.S., 1, 3; G.W., 1, 77 (omitting Breuer's contributions). (xxix, 3–17, 18–20, 22–23, 24–25, 43)

[*Trans.: Studies on Hysteria, Standard Ed.*, 2. Including Breuer's contributions.]

(1900*a*) *Die Traumdeutung*, Vienna. G.S., 2–3; G.W., 2–3. (33–34)

[*Trans.: The Interpretation of Dreams*, London and New York, 1955; *Standard Ed.*, 4–5.]

(1901*b*) *Zur Psychopathologie des Alltagslebens*, Berlin, 1904. G.S., 4, 3; G.W., 4. (39)

[*Trans.: The Psychopathology of Everyday Life, Standard Ed.*, 6.]

(1904*a*) 'Die Freud'sche psychoanalytische Methode', G.S., 6, 3; G.W., 5, 3. (63)

[*Trans.:* 'Freud's Psycho-Analytic Procedure', C.P., 1, 264; *Standard Ed.*, 7, 249.]

(1905*a*) 'Über Psychotherapie', G.S., 6, 11; G.W., 5, 13. (63)

[*Trans.:* 'On Psychotherapy', C.P., 1, 249; *Standard Ed.*, 7, 257.]

(1905*c*) *Der Witz und seine Beziehung zum Unbewussten*, Vienna. G.S., 9, 5; G.W., 6. (30–31)

[*Trans.: Jokes and their Relation to the Unconscious, Standard Ed.*, 8.]

(1905*d*) *Drei Abhandlungen zur Sexualtheorie*, Vienna. G.S., 5, 3; G.W., 5, 29. (45, 46)

[*Trans.: Three Essays on the Theory of Sexuality*, London, 1949; *Standard Ed.*, 7, 125.]

(1906*a*) 'Meine Ansichten über die Rolle der Sexualität in der Ätiologie der Neurosen', G.S., 5, 123; G.W., 5, 149. (63)

[*Trans.:* 'My Views on the Part played by Sexuality in the Aetiology of the Neuroses', C.P., 1, 272; *Standard Ed.*, 7, 271.]

(1909*b*) 'Analyse der Phobie eines fünfjährigen Knaben', G.S., 8, 129; G.W., 7, 243. (46)

[*Trans.:* 'Analysis of a Phobia in a Five-Year-Old Boy', C.P., 3, 149; *Standard Ed.*, 10, 3.]

(1910*a* [1909]) *Über Psychoanalyse*, Vienna. G.S., 4, 349; G.W., 8, 3. (63)

[*Trans.:* 'Five Lectures on Psycho-Analysis', Amer. J. Psychol., 21 (1910), 181; *Standard Ed.*, 11, 3.]

(1910*h*) 'Über einen besonderen Typus der Objektwahl beim Manne', G.S., 5, 186; G.W., 8, 66. (51)

[*Trans.:* 'A Special Type of Choice of Object made by Men', *C.P.*, 4, 192; *Standard Ed.*, 11, 165.]

(1913*j*) 'Das Interesse an der Psychoanalyse', *G.S.*, 4, 313; *G.W.*, 8, 390. (63)

[*Trans.:* 'The Claims of Psycho-Analysis to Scientific Interest', *Standard Ed.*, 13, 165.]

(1913*m* [1911]) 'On Psycho-Analysis' [in English], *Aust. med. Congr.* (Transactions of the Ninth Session, held in Sydney, New South Wales, Sept. 1911), 2, Part 8, 839; *Standard Ed.*, 12. (63)

(1914*d*) 'Zur Geschichte der psychoanalytischen Bewegung', *G.S.*, 4, 411; *G.W.*, 10, 44. (xxviii, 3, 63)

[*Trans.:* 'On the History of the Psycho-Analytic Movement', *C.P.*, 1, 287; *Standard Ed.*, 14, 3.]

(1916–17) *Vorlesungen zur Einführung in die Psychoanalyse*, Vienna. *G.S.*, 7; *G.W.*, 11. (xxix, 63)

[*Trans.: Introductory Lectures on Psycho-Analysis*, revised ed., London, 1929 (*A General Introduction to Psychoanalysis*, New York, 1935); *Standard Ed.*, 15–16.]

(1923*a*) ' "Psychoanalyse" und "Libido Theorie" ', *G.S.*, 11, 201; *G.W.*, 13, 211. (63)

[*Trans.:* 'Two Encyclopaedia Articles', *C.P.*, 5, 107; *Standard Ed.*, 18, 235.]

(1924*f*) 'A Short Account of Psycho-Analysis' [published as 'Psychoanalysis: Exploring the Hidden Recesses of the Mind'], Chap. 73, Vol. 2 of *These Eventful Years*, London and New York; *Standard Ed.*, 19. (63)

[*German Text:* 'Kurzer Abriss der Psychoanalyse', *G.S.*, 11, 183; *G.W.*, 13, 405. German original first appeared in 1928.]

(1925*d* [1924]) *Selbstdarstellung*, Vienna, 1934. *G.S.*, 11, 119; *G.W.*, 14, 33. (xxviii, 63)

[*Trans.: An Autobiographical Study*, London, 1935 (*Autobiography*, New York, 1935); *Standard Ed.*, 20.]

(1925*g*) 'Josef Breuer', *G.S.*, 11, 281; *G.W.*, 14, 562. (3)

[*Trans.:* 'Josef Breuer', *Int. J. Psycho-Anal.*, 6, 459; *Standard Ed.*, 19.]

(1926*e*) *Die Frage der Laienanalyse*, Vienna. *G.S.*, 11, 307; *G.W.*, 14, 209. (63)

[*Trans.: The Question of Lay Analysis*, London, 1947; *Standard Ed.*, 20.]

(1926*f*) An Article in the *Encyclopaedia Britannica* [published as 'Psycho-Analysis: Freudian School'], *Encyclopaedia Britannica*, 13th ed., New Vol. 3, 253; *Standard Ed.*, 20. (63)

[*German Text:* 'Psycho-Analysis', *G.S.*, 12, 372; *G.W.*, 14, 299. German original first appeared in 1934.]

(1933*a*) *Neue Folge der Vorlesungen zur Einführung in die Psychoanalyse*, Vienna. *G.S.*, 12, 151; *G.W.*, 15, 207. (64)

[*Trans.: New Introductory Lectures on Psycho-Analysis*, London and New York, 1933; *Standard Ed.*, 22.]

(1940*a* [1938]) *Abriss der Psychoanalyse*, *G.W.*, 17, 67. (64)

[*Trans.: An Outline of Psycho-Analysis*, London and New York, 1949; *Standard Ed.*, 23.]

(1940*b* [1938]) 'Some Elementary Lessons in Psycho-Analysis' [title in English: German text], *G.W.*, 17, 141. (64)

[*Trans.:* 'Some Elementary Lessons in Psycho-Analysis', *C.P.*, 5, 376; *Standard Ed.*, 23.]

JONES, E. (1955) *Sigmund Freud: Life and Work*, Vol. 2, London and New York. (xxviii)

JUNG, C. G. (1906) (ed.) *Diagnostische Assoziationsstudien*, Leipzig. (32–33)

[*Trans.: Studies in Word-Association*, London, 1918.]

(1910) 'Über Konflikte der kindlichen Seele', *Jb. psychoan. psychopath. Forsch.*, 2, 33. (46)

LINDNER, S. (1879) 'Das Saugen an den Fingern, Lippen, etc., bei den Kindern (Ludeln)', *Jb. Kinderheilk.*, N.F., 14, 68. (47)

RANK, O. (1907) *Der Künstler*, Vienna. (56)

(1909) *Der Mythus von der Geburt des Helden*, Vienna. (171)

[*Trans.: The Myth of the Birth of the Hero*, New York, 1914.]

GENERAL INDEX

This index includes the names of non-technical authors. It also includes the names of technical authors where no reference is made in the text to specific works. For references to specific technical works; the Bibliography should be consulted.